Except where otherwise noted, all scripture quotations are taken from the **King James Version** of the Bible.

RISE AND BE HEALED

ISBN - 978-978-48067-9-4

Copyright 2011 © Victor Adeyemi

Printed in USA

All rights reserved. No part of this publication may be reproduced, stored in a retrieval system, or transmitted in any form or by any means - electronic, mechanical, photocopying, recording, or otherwise – without the prior written permission of the publisher and copyright owners.

CONTENTS

ACKNOWLEDGMENT

Several peoples input made this book possible and their invaluable contributions are highly appreciated. Thanks to the Global Harvest Church Ibadan where I held my first ever HEALING SCHOOL, which materials formed the substance of the book.

Kenneth E. Hagin's teachings opened my eyes to the reality of divine healing. Most of what I know derives from his exceptional teaching ministry.

Benny Hinn remains one of my greatest inspirations in the healing ministry. I am thankful for the impartations received through his videos, television programmes, books and the laying on of his hands at his crusades.

My gratitude to Ope Elegbede for transcribing the messages and offering her kind advices.

Pastors Segun Oke and Tolu Aladesanmi edited the book. Your hard work can only be rewarded in eternity. Thank you for giving to the Lord.

I am also thankful for the support of Dare Kolawole, my Executive Assistant in supervising the entire process.

Many thanks to Pastor Kayode Ijisesan and his wonderful staff at KingsWord International Church, Chicago for beautifully repackaging the book.

Without the encouragement and constant inspiration I get from Jumoke, my darling wife, this book wouldn't have seen the light of day. I love you more than life itself. I am also thankful for the love of our four wonderful children.

Finally, to Jehovah Rapha, The Lord that healeth me, be glory, honor, adoration and dominion forever.

Introduction

My childhood and teenage years were characterized by constant sickness. It is said that Malaria fever is the second deadliest disease ravaging the continent of Africa and killing her young.

Thanks to the discovery of quinine, else the likes of me would have been annihilated in our prime. Yet the quinine drugs would cause terrible allergies especially itching, so much that I dreaded the itching more than the fever itself. Life was therefore hellish until I came to Christ and encountered believers who lived without regular sickness and even when sick, looked up to God for healing. The prospect of living without quinine was a major reason for my interest in the subject of divine healing.

My discovery from Kenneth Hagin's books and several others changed my perspective and led me to the wonderful experience of God's healing power. My interest in healing has remained till this day. It is my pleasure to share my knowledge as a contribution to the many written before mine, in the hope that someone without access to my sources but within my circle of influence might experience the same spiritual encounters I have found through the healing power of God and His powerful word.

Chapter 1
The Origin of Sickness

"And the LORD God said unto the woman, what is this that thou hast done? And the woman said, the serpent beguiled me, and I did eat. And the LORD God said unto the serpent, Because thou hast done this, thou art cursed above all cattle, and above every beast of the field; upon thy belly shalt thou go, and dust shalt thou eat all the days of thy life: And I will put enmity between thee and the woman, and between thy seed and her seed; it shall bruise thy head, and thou shalt bruise his heel. Unto the woman he said, I will greatly multiply thy sorrow and thy conception; in sorrow thou shalt bring forth children; and thy desire shall be to thy husband, and he shall rule over thee. And unto Adam he said, because thou hast hearkened unto the voice of thy wife, and hast eaten of the tree, of which I commanded thee, saying, Thou shalt not eat of it: cursed is the ground for thy sake; in sorrow shalt thou eat of it all the days of thy life; Thorns also and thistles shall it bring forth to thee; and thou shalt eat the herb of the field; In the sweat of thy face shalt thou eat bread, till thou return unto the ground; for out of

it wast thou taken: for dust thou art, and unto dust shalt thou return." **Genesis 3:13-19**

In chapter 3 of the book of Genesis, we find the story of the fall of man. But according to Genesis 1:26-27, God created man in His own image, essence, nature; and likeness. And in God's image there is no sickness. The state of sickness is a state of imperfection. Sickness is a state of disrepair. It is a state of malfunction or dysfunction. So when a person is sick, all is not well. When you are sick, you don't feel good. That doesn't look like the image of God and it doesn't depict God's likeness at all.

God certainly made man perfect. Genesis 1:31 tells us about the state of all God's creation; when He made them. And the Bible records:

"And God saw everything that he had made, and, behold, it was very good. And the evening and the morning were the sixth day."

The expression "very good" here could as well mean perfect. Some translations actually uses the word "perfect". Our God is a God of excellence. Everything He does, He does excellently.

"O LORD our Lord, how excellent is thy name in all the earth!"
Psalm 8:9

So, when God created man, He created Him perfectly. There was nothing imperfect in man's creation. Sometimes people get confused by Genesis 2:18, where God said it wasn't good for the man to be alone. Yes, the loneliness was not good, but the man himself was perfect. Otherwise, the woman God made would not have perfected him either, because she was made out of him.

Let's note the following points:

1. **God made man perfect**. He made him perfect and holy, without sickness or disease. He made him pain free – all his organs and systems were functioning. His heart pumped blood perfectly, his kidneys carried out their functions perfectly. Everything was absolutely normal and working right.

2. **Pain was first mentioned in the Bible after sin**. In other words, before man sinned, there was no mention of pain or sickness. It was after man sinned that God made those declarations we read in Genesis 3. This marked the entrance of pain and sickness into the world. God spoke to the woman and said in verse 16 of Genesis 3:

   "Unto the woman he said, I will greatly multiply thy sorrow and thy conception; in sorrow thou shall bring forth children; and thy desire shall be to thy husband, and he shall rule over thee."

Of course, it is impossible for a baby to come into the world through the birth canal without the woman feeling some pain and inconvenience. But it is apparent from this verse of Scripture that it was not intended to be what it has become. I have been in the labor ward a few times for the birth of my children and it's not just easy at all. It's a very painful process. The multiplication of the pains of child birth came after sin. God never intended for women to go through so much pain.

Now in verse 17, God spoke to Adam:

> *"And unto Adam he said, Because thou hast hearkened unto the voice of thy wife, and hast eaten of the tree, of which I commanded thee, saying, Thou shall not eat of it: cursed is the ground for thy sake; in sorrow shall thou eat of it all the days of thy life;"*

God said man came from dust and to it he will return, meaning that his body will disintegrate. Through sickness, his body will fall apart. God made the pronouncement that guaranteed sickness and disease would come into the world as a consequence of sin.

Even though the human body was not meant to disintegrate as we see in Genesis 3:22:

"And the LORD God said, Behold, the man is become as one of us, to know good and evil: and now, lest he put forth his hand, and take also of the tree of life, and eat, and live forever:"

The original plan of God was that man should live forever. Remember that God said he could eat of the fruit of any tree in the garden except that of the knowledge of good and evil.

That meant that man was free to eat of the tree of life, which would make him live forever. If he had tasted of the fruit of that tree, he would never have been able to fall sick or die. He would have lived forever. God's intention was for you and me to be born into this world and live here forever. So the disintegration of the human body was pronounced, and came into operation after sin entered into the world.

This was so because God had warned them earlier, when He gave man commandments on how to manage the garden; that he should not touch the tree of the knowledge of good and evil.

"But of the tree of the knowledge of good and evil, thou shalt not eat of it: for in the day that thou eatest thereof thou shalt surely die."
Genesis 2:17

In other words, "the day you eat of it, you sin and you die". The consequence in particular was that the principle of death was brought into operation; and death is a consequence of sin. It is automatic.

The reason why sickness came was because death came. As drizzles are to rain, so is sickness to death. Sickness is the inception of death into the body. It is the arrival of death in the body. As the *rider* is to a president, so is sickness to death. When you see a convoy of protocol and security men, you know it's a signal to the presence of an important personality. Sickness is a manifestation of death. Death conveys pictures of cessation of existence: total annihilation from this world is what comes to mind.

However, death can manifest itself in a gradual way and sicknesses, diseases, and infections are manifestations of death. So sin and death go together. One cannot have one without the other. Once you get the water, you get the "wet" automatically. So wherever sin is found, death is found there also. When Adam opened the door to sin, he automatically opened the door to death. Romans 6:23 says:

"For the wages of sin is death; but the gift of God is eternal life through Jesus Christ our Lord."

And Romans 8:2 also says:

"For the law of the Spirit of life in Christ Jesus hath made me free from the law of sin and death."

When put together, it is not two laws, but one. The law of sin and death is a law that has two sides to it. Once you have the first side, the second automatically follows. Sin and death are two sides of the same coin. Sin opens the door for death to manifest itself, and sickness is the inception or arrival of death. That's why sickness and disease should not be toyed with. I have challenges with those who believe that sickness is the will of God and that at times God uses sickness to punish or discipline His children.

We will certainly touch on this later on in this book, but it is lack of proper understanding of God and Scriptures that make people believe and say things like "Everything is the will of God." Whatever happens, they say it's the "Will of God". Statements like "The Lord giveth, the Lord taketh, blessed be the name of the Lord" are used when people die of certain illnesses and diseases. But for some, may be if they had lived a healthier lifestyle, quit smoking or womanizing; just may be, they would be alive.

3. **Satan is responsible for sin, and consequently sickness.** All sin originated from the devil. There was no sin before it was found in Satan. In fact, in Ezekiel 28, referring to Satan himself, the Scripture reads in verse 15:

"Thou wast perfect in thy ways from the day that thou wast created, till iniquity was found in thee."

The first time iniquity was found, it was found in Satan. He is the source of all sin and iniquity. In Genesis 3, he was the one who tempted Eve; he then used her to tempt Adam to sin against God. The moment they sinned, they opened the door for death to come in. Like I said earlier, once you have the first one, the second automatically follows.

The same is found in the book of James chapter 1; it spells out the process of sin:

"Let no man say when he is tempted, I am tempted of God: for God cannot be tempted with evil, neither tempteth he any man: But every man is tempted, when he is drawn away of his own lust, and enticed. Then when lust hath conceived, it bringeth forth sin: and sin, when it is finished, bringeth forth death."
James 1:13-15

Now death is the end of sin; and the reason why Satan caused sin to come in, was so that death could come in. Death is an operation of Satan. Sin opened the door for Satan to operate. In Ephesians 4, we are told in verse 33 to be angry, but to sin not. The Bible tells us not to allow bitterness, resentment and such things in our lives; verse 27 says **"and neither give place to the devil"**. The reality is that sin gives place to the devil. Sin opens the door to Satan and permits his operation in our lives. It gives Satan a foothold or legal right to operate – It licenses the devil.

In Acts 10:38, sickness is described as an oppression of the devil:

> *"How God anointed Jesus of Nazareth with the Holy Ghost and with power: who went about doing good, and healing **all that were oppressed of the devil**; for God was with him."*

Sickness is described as satanic activity. Sicknesses and diseases do not come from God. Satan is the author of all sickness and disease; and we must understand that sickness and diseases are oppressions of the devil. It was the devil that brought them into the world to oppress us. So when you see sickness and disease in your body, know that it is satanic activity; don't welcome it. Don't endorse it or view it as normal. When it comes to your definition of the norm, or what you see as fit and proper, let it be what you find in Genesis 2.

Myles Munroe is fond of saying that Genesis chapter 1 and 2 are the only perfect chapters in the Bible; because it's in these chapters that we find the originality of God's creation in perfection. The moment you get to chapter 3, you find sin; and after that, its consequences. So he says that everything God began to do from Genesis 3 till Revelation 21 is to get us back to Genesis 1 and 2. Sin opens the door to Satan, who is the afflicter of men. The Bible records in the Book of Job, the second chapter and the seventh verse:

"So went Satan forth from the presence of the LORD, and smote Job with sore boils from the sole of his foot unto his crown."

When you see boil on your body, know that it didn't come from God. So don't welcome the boil. There's a Nigerian superstition that when you see a boil on your body it means money is coming your way. Don't be deceived; all sicknesses are signs of death – the disintegration of man's body and a cessation of life. Don't welcome the infection, but fight and destroy it. Get rid of it by every means available within God's will. Of course, we discover in Scriptures, even in the New Testament, that the devil is responsible for certain sicknesses:

"And he was teaching in one of the synagogues on the Sabbath. And, behold, there was a woman which had a spirit of infirmity eighteen years, and was bowed together, and could in no wise lift up herself."
Luke 13:10-11

The woman walked around bent in half, and there was nothing normal about it. I'm sure the doctors of this age would have their explanations for her condition, but the Bible records that she had a spirit of infirmity. That was the root of her situation and when Jesus saw her:

> *"… He called her to him, and said unto her, Woman, thou art loosed from thine infirmity. And he laid his hands on her: and immediately she was made straight, and glorified God. And the ruler of the synagogue answered with indignation, because that Jesus had healed on the Sabbath day, and said unto the people, There are six days in which men ought to work: in them therefore come and be healed, and not on the Sabbath day. The Lord then answered him, and said, Thou hypocrite, doth not each one of you on the Sabbath loose his ox or his ass from the stall, and lead him away to watering? And ought not this woman, being a daughter of Abraham, whom Satan hath bound, lo, these eighteen years, be loosed from this bond on the Sabbath day?"*
> **Luke 13:12-16**

When a demon spirit is in operation, it is in operation on behalf of Satan. ***"Whom Satan hath bound lo these eighteen years… "*** Satan bound her. It was a demonic operation of darkness going on here. It was not of God, it was the devil doing it and God absolutely had nothing to do with it. Remember again Acts 10:38, *"How God anointed Jesus of Nazareth with the Holy Ghost and with power: who went about doing good, and healing all that were oppressed of the devil; for God was with him."* Sickness is satanic oppression.

In Mark 9:17-18, we see the story of a boy who needed deliverance:

"And one of the multitude answered and said, Master, I have brought unto thee my son, which hath a dumb spirit; And wheresoever he taketh him, he teareth him: and he foameth, and gnasheth with his teeth, and pineth away: and I spake to thy disciples that they should cast him out; and they could not."

This situation is a condition medical science knows as epilepsy. It is said to be a problem of the nervous system, but it has a spiritual background. That's why epilepsy defies natural and medical solutions. The reality is that it is a spiritual problem.

I remember a young man coming to me in Ilorin, Kwara State, Nigeria in 1990 telling me about this problem. I told him I believed it was spiritual and I laid hands on him and commanded the devil to leave in Jesus name. After the demon left, the epilepsy left. The last I knew of him was that he had become a young minister of the gospel, totally free from epilepsy. I also remember a young lady in Ado-Ekiti, Nigeria years ago. I held a meeting there, probably in year 2000 or 2001. She had the same condition and the epilepsy stopped immediately the devil was out of her. Praise God!

"And ofttimes it hath cast him into the fire, and into the waters, to destroy him: but if thou canst do any thing, have compassion on us, and help us… When Jesus saw that the people came running together, he rebuked the foul spirit, saying unto him, Thou dumb and deaf spirit, I charge thee, come out of him, and enter no more into him. And the spirit cried, and rent him sore, and

came out of him: and he was as one dead; insomuch that many said, He is dead. But Jesus took him by the hand, and lifted him up; and he arose."
Mark 9:22,25-27

From these two stories, we can see that demons were responsible for the sicknesses. So Satan is behind all sicknesses and diseases. Sickness and disease originated from Satan through sin. Sin opened the door for the devil to enter, and that was how sickness began. That's still how sicknesses and diseases are perpetuated today – they are satanic activities.

Now it doesn't necessarily mean that when you see someone sick or you notice symptoms of sickness in your body, then there's a demon in your body. No; not necessarily. In later chapters, you will come to understand that it's not all sicknesses that have demons behind them, but some do; especially those that defy medical help and attention.

There are times when a condition is medically curable, but for certain people, it is just incurable. They apply all the drugs and therapies available in the world, yet the sickness or disease stays in their bodies and refuse to go. For this kind of situation, you've got to understand that there's something else behind it. At times some cancers are due to the presence of evil spirits.

A few years ago I was ministering at Living Word Fellowship in Newport News, Virginia – a church led by a friend. I'll never forget this particular lady, who had diabetes combined with partial blindness and heart trouble. She had a combination of about 3 deadly ailments put together. When I laid hands on her, there was a demonic manifestation and I knew it was a demon spirit behind her condition. So I rebuked the devil and by the word of knowledge I knew it was the spirit of death in her. At times it's the spirit of death operating with some other demons. This was a case of the spirit of death operating with the spirit of infirmity. It was death trying to use infirmity to destroy her life. So, I commanded the spirit to leave in Jesus name. Not long after, she was looking normal and fresh and was so excited at how wonderful she felt. All her pains disappeared.

Again, I was ministering at Student's Christian Movement, University of Ibadan, Nigeria; this was in 1991, at The Chapel of Resurrection. After praying for the sick, I took some testimonies; and a young lady came out and said "for five years I have been very sick. I'm always sick and have been that way for the last five years of my life". She was trembling but she continued and said, "I saw a demon go out of me". I asked, "You saw a demon go out of you?" She answered, "Yes. Its body was like that of a ram." She was really trembling but was completely healed of all her illnesses.

I used to have a spiritual daughter, years ago in Ilorin, Kwara State, Nigeria. She later was made whole and became a pastor; but at a time she was troubled by the spirit of infirmity. She had several ailments. At every point in time, there were at least two of them in manifestation in her body. She had problems with her eyes and wore very thick glasses. She had ulcer, terrible dysmenorrheal, appendicitis, migraine headache, and rheumatism. And once it rained, her bones were in trouble. She also had regular malaria fever. But she was delivered. Praise God!

4. **The absence of God opens the door to Satan.** Every time I preach and make reference to this point, it reminds me of a Nigerian yoruba adage that says "The absence of the cat has turned the house into a den of rats." Rats don't hang around whenever the cat is found. Separation from God removes His divine protection from our lives.

Psalm 91:1 says:

"He that dwelleth in the secret place of the Most High shall abide under the shadow of the Almighty."

When you're not in the secret place, you're simply not under the shadow and the protection of the Almighty. The absence of God brings satanic presence. Once the light was withdrawn from the earth because of the flood of God's judgment between Genesis 1:1 and Genesis 1:2; darkness filled everywhere. In verse 3, God said *"let there be light..."*, and the light pushed the darkness back. The light dispelled the darkness. Light is symbolic of God's presence and activity, while darkness is symbolic of satanic presence and activity.

Chapter 2
Healing in the Atonement

The atoning work of Christ on the cross of Calvary is the heart of the Christian message. The first Adam plunged humanity into sin, but the last Adam (Jesus) came to reverse it, by sacrificing His life to atone for the sins of the whole world. Healing is a part of His work of atonement.

"Who hath believed our report? And to whom is the arm of the LORD revealed? For he shall grow up before him as a tender plant, and as a root out of a dry ground: he hath no form or comeliness; and when we shall see him, there is no beauty that we should desire him. He is despised and rejected of men; a man of sorrows, and acquainted with grief: and we hid as it were our faces from him; he was despised, and we esteemed him not. Surely he hath borne our griefs, and carried our sorrows: yet we did esteem him stricken, smitten of God, and afflicted. But he was wounded for our transgressions; he was bruised for our iniquities: the chastisement of our peace was

upon him; and with his stripes we are healed. All we like sheep have gone astray; we have turned every one to his own way; and the LORD hath laid on him the iniquity of us all."
Isaiah 53:1-6

This is the story of the atoning work of Christ. The word "atonement" itself means *appeasement*. It means to appease. A man does wrong and is told to make an appeasement for his wrong. Wherever or whenever covenant is broken, there is need for atonement.

When God allowed the Babylonians to conquer Israel and carry all its citizens to Babylon as slaves, there was such a terrible destruction of the city and desecration of the temple; only a small remnant was left in Israel. The extent of the destruction made the surrounding nations wonder at what the sin of Israel could have been to warrant such waste and destruction. According to the book of Isaiah, the answer to these nations was that the people of Israel had abandoned their God. These nations were idol worshipers who didn't know the God of Israel; so their perception of the situation was that Israel had stopped sacrificing to her *god*.

They saw it in the light of idol worship. While what they said was true, their perception of the God of Israel was wrong because He wasn't just a god, He was (and still is) the God of gods, the true God of all the earth.

But what they said was true. Israel abandoned her God. Every god that is worshipped has demands. When you have a covenant with a god, there are demands based on that covenant – even if it is an evil one.

Our fore-fathers in Africa worshipped idols and those idols made demands on them. There were things they were to sacrifice. At times in some communities, life has to be sacrificed and blood has to be shed. For some, it's the blood of chickens, or rams, or goats; and if the covenant is abandoned and neglected, the god (which is really a satanic spirit) goes angry and reacts.So when there's a covenant relationship, there are always covenant demands. At a time, things were not going well in Israel. God had to send a prophet to tell them why. He sent prophet Malachi; who told them that their first problem was their irreverence in the worship of God.

The second problem of the nation was that their men were dealing treacherously with their wives. And the third was that they were robbing God in tithes and offerings. If the nation will correct herself in these areas and live up to the terms of the covenant, the nation will be blessed once again. That's why atonement is necessary.

God, right from the beginning, has always intended to have a covenant relationship with man.

Inherent in the blessing of Genesis 1:28 was covenant, when He said *"be fruitful, multiply, and replenish the earth and subdue it!"* While it was a blessing, it was also a responsibility. God gave man the responsibility to take care of the planet and keep the devil at bay. God used the word "subdue" because the devil was already here. God was literally saying to man, "There will be opposition in the planet, but I've given you the authority, the right and all the power you need to take charge and to take control; so take charge and take control". Instead, man sold out to God's archenemy, the devil. God got angry and wiped out everyone and everything with a flood in the days of Noah, when iniquity multiplied.

However, as soon as Noah and his family were restored by God in Genesis 8, God renewed His covenant with them. He renewed with them the covenant He had made to man initially. Not too long after, sin multiplied again and God finally chose a man by the name Abraham and decided to deal with him and his family alone. God decided that both a natural and a spiritual nation would come out of Abraham, and today we are the seed of Abraham.

> *"And if ye be Christ's, then are ye Abraham's seed, and heirs according to the promise."*
> **Galatians 3:29**

Like I mentioned earlier, there are demands to every

covenant, and there are conditions that have to be met. From the moment man sinned against God, an atonement for the sins of humanity became a necessity. However, there was no life qualified to atone for the sins of humanity, so God made do with an interim arrangement. He instantly killed an animal, took its skin with the wet blood and wrapped it around Adam and Eve so that the blood could appease Him and the life of the animal could represent that of the man. As time went on, we see this being established in the old covenant.

In the old covenant, God said in Exodus 12, that every family of Israel was to take a lamb, and they were to kill it for the family, take the blood, and put it on lintels, side posts and doors of their houses. **"When I see the blood, I will pass over"** God said.

Later, God commanded them to kill a lamb for the whole nation. The high priest was to offer the blood of the lamb on behalf of the whole nation. Initially, it was one lamb for one man; later it became one lamb for one family, and eventually one lamb for a whole nation. But all the sacrifices we see in the Old Testament – all the pigeon, goat and ram sacrifices – were all symbolic of the real Lamb of God that would be sacrificed for the sins of the whole world. Not just for one man, or a family, or a whole nation, but for the whole world!

That lamb was the person of Jesus Christ. In going to Calvary's cross and shedding His blood, He laid down His life to appease the God who had been betrayed by humanity. His blood atoned for the past, present and future sins of humanity. On Calvary's cross He paid that price once and for all.

> *"For the life of the flesh is in the blood: and I have given it to you upon the altar to make an atonement for your souls: for it is the blood that maketh an atonement for the soul."*
> **Leviticus 17:11**

Only blood can make atonement for sin. Hence, the blood of Jesus was shed to make atonement for our sins. Once the blood of Jesus was shed, God was appeased.

In the Atoning Work of Christ:

1.   **Christ was made sin for us.** That was how His work of atonement for us took place. All our sins were laid on Him like we read in Isaiah 53:6:

> *"All we like sheep have gone astray; we have turned everyone to his own way; and the LORD hath laid on him the iniquity of us all."*

All the sins we've ever committed and would ever commit were laid on Jesus. But any sin that is not genuinely repented of is not taken care of by the cross. Repentance is the condition for forgiveness (I John 1:9).

God cannot be deceived though; if a person repents of a sin with the intention to go back into it, it is not forgiven. In the case of genuine repentance, the blood of Jesus shed on Calvary's cross is a powerful and efficacious sacrifice once and for all, for the atonement of sins.

That's why we have the first Adam according to 1 Corinthians 15, and Jesus is known as the last Adam. He is the last and not the second Adam because after Him there won't be another one. When He hung on that cross and said "it is finished", what He meant was, there would never be a sacrifice for sin any more. Glory be to God! The work that was performed on the cross was a perfect one. Jesus' blood is more than sufficient for us. In 2 Corinthians 5:21, the Bible says:

> "For he hath made him to be sin for us, who knew no sin; that we might be made the righteousness of God in him"

We read in Isaiah 53:5:

> "But he was wounded for our transgressions; he was bruised for our iniquities: the chastisement of our peace was upon him; and with his stripes we are healed."

1 Peter 2:24 also says:

"Who his own self bare our sins in his own body on the tree, that we, being dead to sins, should live unto righteousness: by whose stripes ye were healed."

The word *"bare"* here means to carry vicariously; or to carry on behalf of another. When Jesus went to the cross, He went as our substitute and He received and carried the punishment that was due for our sins - the death due to us because of our sins. He died on our behalf. As far as God was concerned, when He hung on the cross and was killed, you were killed. When life was snuffed out of Him, life was drawn out of you. All the punishment that He received, He received on our behalf.

As far as God is concerned, you have received the punishment for your sins. The price for everything you ever did and will ever do by way of sin has been paid for on that cross. God reckons it as though you yourself paid for your sins. Of course you didn't do it yourself. Somebody did it on your behalf, but God counts it to your record. When someone pays your debt on your behalf, you don't owe the debt anymore. Jesus paid all our debt on the cross of Calvary.

Not only did He shed His blood to pay the debt we owed God; He also paid the devil and every idol that our ancestors worshiped. There is still so much fear of generational curses because of what our ancestors worshipped; but when the blood of our redemption was shed, it was shed to redeem us from their hands also. All the covenant debt that your ancestors and your family owe to any idol has been paid for – the blood paid for everything. Their legal right to oppress you is taken away. They don't have any right to touch your life or to operate in your life anymore. You can plead the blood of Jesus against them.

The blood of Jesus is enough argument to silence the powers of darkness. No child of God should be afraid of the operation of the forces of darkness. It doesn't matter whatever was worshipped in your family, the blood of Jesus has paid the price for your freedom. You can plead the blood of Jesus against that thing, and it must shut its mouth!

Jesus today is our righteousness; because He did a *substitutionary* work for us on the cross. He took our place, so that we could take His place. He took our sins, so we could have His righteousness, like we read in 1 Peter 2:24.

There was an exchange that took place on the cross. If it was sin that opened the door for Satan, and our sins have been taken by the Lord Jesus Christ, then Satan has lost his legal right to afflict you, and to operate in your life. He lost it, Hallelujah!

"In whom also ye are circumcised with the circumcision made without hands, in putting off the body of the sins of the flesh by the circumcision of Christ:"
Colossians 2:11

Circumcision was the only way a male child could become a seed of Abraham and an heir of the covenant God made with Abraham in the Old Testament. By saying that we have been circumcised here, it means that we have been brought into covenant with God and have become heirs; howbeit, this circumcision is not physical; but the putting away of the body of sin by the circumcision of Christ.

"Buried with him in baptism, wherein also ye are risen with him through the faith of the operation of God, who hath raised him from the dead. And you, being dead in your sins and the uncircumcision of your flesh, hath he quickened together with him, having forgiven you all trespasses; Blotting out the hand-writing of ordinances that was against us, which was contrary to us, and took it out of the way, nailing it to his cross;"
Colossians 2:12-14

Verse 14 is usually used in claiming deliverance; but while this is appropriate, the context in which it was used is different. The word "ordinances" speaks of the law - referring to the Old Testament Laws of Moses. Without a law there is no offence. The law was given so that there might be offence.

So the Bible now says that "everything written against us was blotted out. How? - By nailing them to the cross.

> *"And having spoiled principalities and powers, he made a shew of them openly, triumphing over them in it."*
> **Colossians 2:15**

Satan has lost all his legal right to touch your life. Any operation of Satan that takes place in your life as a believer, including the operation of sickness, is unlawful; it is illegal.

2.   **He bore our sicknesses also.** In the verses we've looked at, we see that Jesus did not only bear our sins and their punishment; He took our sicknesses also. He was wounded for our transgressions, and bruised for our iniquities. He got the punishment due for our sins; He also got the punishment due to us for our healing:

> *"But he was wounded for our transgressions, he was bruised for our iniquities: the chastisement of our peace was upon him; and with his stripes we are healed."*
> **Isaiah 53:5**

Stripes were laid on Him for our healing. He paid the price not only for sin, but also for the consequences of sin.

"Who his own self bare our sins in his own body on the tree, that we, being dead to sins, should live unto righteousness: by whose stripes ye were healed."
1 Peter 2:24

"That it might be fulfilled which was spoken by Esaias the prophet, saying, Himself took our infirmities, and bare our sicknesses."
Matthew 8:17

The world "took" here means to carry on behalf of. The words *"took"* and *"bare"* are from the same root and mean the same thing. He carried of our sins and sicknesses so we would not have to carry them anymore. When you see symptoms of sickness in your body, they are just lying against the truth - it is an illegal operation. They are operating illegally and it is an attempt by Satan to cheat you. Jesus already carried your sicknesses and diseases. The work of redemption broke every legal ground upon which the devil could afflict you.

3.   He redeemed us from the curse of the law.
Galatians 3:13 says:

"Christ hath redeemed us from the curse of the law, being made a curse for us: for it is written, Cursed is every one that hangeth on a tree:"

What is the curse of the law? In Deuteronomy 28:15-68, we find the entire curse that will serve as consequences for not obeying the law. We find boils, migraine headache, poverty, fever, failure and all manners of evil there (verses 22-27). Jesus carried all these things for us on the cross; so we don't need to carry them anymore. If you find any of these things in your life, just know that it's the devil cheating you. You've got to put a stop to his operation in your life.

4.   He conquered death for us. He fought and conquered death, so that death will lose its power. If He didn't conquer death, then how did he rise from the dead? On the third day, Jesus rose again because he had conquered death. In Revelation 1:18, He said:

"I am he that liveth, and was dead; and, behold, I am alive for evermore, Amen; and have the keys of hell and of death."

Jesus is now in control of death because He has the keys. Hell cannot hold just anybody it wants anymore; death cannot kill just anyone it wants anymore. Jesus said, "I've got the keys," and we established earlier that sickness is the inception of death in the body. But Romans 8:2 says:

"For the law of the Spirit of life in Christ Jesus hath made me free from the law of sin and death."

We are therefore free, Hallelujah!

> *"Forasmuch then as the children are partakers of flesh and blood, he also himself likewise took part of the same; that through death he might destroy him that had the power of death, that is, the devil; And deliver them who through fear of death were all their lifetime subject to bondage."*
> **Hebrews 2:14-15**

Jesus tasted death so that He could destroy him who had the power over death. So He destroyed the devil, all principalities and powers, and the spirit of death. He overcame death so you could overcome also.

> *"O death, where is thy sting? O grave, where is thy victory?"*
> **1 Corinthians 15:55**

Since He took care of sin, death is taken care of also. Sin is the sting of death, and He took it away on the cross. It was sin that gave death the right to afflict us; and it was the law that presented the opportunity for sin to come in because without the law there is no sin. So He took the law out (Colossians 2:14) and consequently sin. So death is defeated; glory be to God!

You might want to ask: "So if Jesus took death out, why do people still die?" The answer is: Right now, through divine health, we can enjoy a foretaste of the redemption of our bodies and our victory over death. However, the full enjoyment of the privileges of our redemption has been postponed till Jesus appears again.

> *"For we know that the whole creation groaneth and travaileth in pain together until now. And not only they, but ourselves also, which have the firstfruits of the Spirit, even we ourselves groan within ourselves, waiting for the adoption, to wit, the redemption of our body."*
> **Romans 8:22-23**

Our bodies have not been fully claimed yet. So, divine healing and health are available to us as a way of claiming part of our victory over death.

> *"But if we hope for that we see not, then do we with patience wait for it"*
> **Romans 8:25**

The redemption of our bodies is in the future when Jesus comes again. When Jesus rose from the dead, He had a glorified body; and we are going to be like Him. Our bodies are going to be redeemed and transformed, like that of Jesus Christ. There is a difference between what Jesus was like before He came into the world, what He was like when He was in the world, and what He was like when He rose from the dead. Before He came into the world, He was a spirit being and couldn't operate directly in the natural. *The word* was spirit, but the Bible says in John 1:14: *"…. and the word became flesh"*. He became human like us. He slept, and was limited by space and time like every human being because He had laid aside His glory in heaven.

But when He was resurrected from the dead, He was given a glorified body. That body could operate in the realm of the spirit and in the realm of the natural at the same time. Before He came into the world, He didn't have flesh, bones and blood, but He got all these when He became human. However, He resurrected with only flesh and bones (Luke 24:39). Walls were no barrier for the kind of the body He resurrected with. Though He could be touched and felt by His disciples (John 20:26-27), and He broke bread and ate with them (John 21:12-14), the same body could at the same time, operate in the spirit realm.

> *"Beloved, now are we the sons of God, and it doth not yet appear what we shall be: but we know that, when he shall appear, we shall be like him; for we shall see him as he is."*
> **1 John 3:2**

This is the same type of body we will have when Jesus returns the second time: glorified bodies without physical limitations. There will be no limit to human potential. We'll be able to think and operate like God. Jesus conquered death for us, and our bodies will be fully redeemed when He comes back again. But until He comes, let us enjoy the potential redemption found in divine health. That's our portion right now.

1.   Healing follows the forgiveness of sin. Once there's forgiveness of sin, healing follows; because sin brought sickness into the world.

> *"Is any sick among you? Let him call for the elders of the church; and let them pray over him, anointing him with oil in the name of the Lord: And the prayer of faith shall save the sick, and the Lord shall raise him up; and if he has committed sins, they shall be forgiven him. Confess your faults one to another, and pray one for another, that ye may be healed. The effectual fervent prayer of a righteous man availeth much."*
> **James 5:14-16**

Here we see healing following the forgiveness of sin. When we own up to one another about our wrong doing, and pray for one another to be restored to the Lord, healing follows. Healing follows the forgiveness of sin.

> *"And, behold, men brought in a bed a man which was taken with palsy: and they sought means to bring him in, and to lay him before him. And when they could not find by what way they*

might bring him in because of the multitude, they went upon the housetop, and let him down through the tiling with his couch into the midst before Jesus. And when he saw their faith, he said unto him, Man, thy sins are forgiven thee... Whether is easier, to say, Thy sins be forgiven thee; or to say, Rise up and walk? But that ye may know that the Son of man hath power upon earth to forgive sins, (he said unto the sick of the palsy,) I say unto thee, Arise, and take up thy couch, and go into thine house."

Luke 5:18-20,23-24

We see the same connection between healing and forgiveness here. Jesus forgave the man's sins before declaring him healed. Also in John 5, we see the story of the man Jesus healed by the pool of the Bethesda. The fourteenth verse reads:

"Afterward Jesus findeth him in the temple, and said unto him, Behold, thou art made whole: sin no more, lest a worse thing come unto thee."

So there is a connection between Sin and Sickness.

In Psalm 103:2-3, the Bible also shows that once your sins are forgiven, all diseases are also healed:

"Bless the LORD, O my soul, and forget not all his benefits: Who forgiveth all thine iniquities; who healeth all thy diseases;"

Summarily, there's healing in the atonement. Not only has the atonement taken care of our sins, not only can we be born again because of Jesus' sacrifice on Calvary's cross, we can also be healed because of His sacrifice on that same cross. The work of atonement that Jesus accomplished on the cross was not only to take away our sins, but also to take away the consequences of sin.

Confession

There's healing in the atonement for me. Jesus Christ came into the world. He went to Calvary's cross. He was sacrificed that my sins might be forgiven; and that my sins might be cancelled. He not only died for my sins, He paid the price for my sickness and my disease.

He Himself took my infirmities and bore my sicknesses. The sacrifice of Jesus on Calvary's cross solved the problem of sin for me and solved the problem of sickness also. Bless the Lord oh my soul and all that is within me, bless His holy name.

Chapter 3
How to Receive Healing

We have already established that healing is in the atonement. It is as much provided for, as the forgiveness and cleansing of sin is provided for. Now, we'll look at how to appropriate the healing available to us.

1. Accept Christ as Your Healer.

When salvation is preached, a person is asked to accept Christ as his Lord and Savior. The import of this decision is that you ascribe the salvation of your soul to the atoning work that Christ did on the cross. It means you trust that by what Jesus Christ did on the cross, your sins are forgiven. We take for granted the fact that the work of the cross is not only capable of bringing forgiveness, but also able to bring a cleansing.

By the work of the cross, you can stand before God without any sense of condemnation whatsoever. At that moment when you believed, you accepted Him as Lord and Savior. In the same vein, you need to accept Christ as your healer.

In the Old Testament, in making a covenant with the children of Israel, and expatiating on the covenant, God revealed Himself as Israel's healer. So He revealed a name to them in Exodus 15:26:

> *"And said, If thou wilt diligently hearken to the voice of the LORD thy God, and wilt do that which is right in his sight, and wilt give ear to his commandments, and keep all his statutes, I will put none of these diseases upon thee, which I have brought upon the Egyptians: for I am the LORD that healeth thee."*

Christ is my savior from sin; and He is also my healer from sicknesses and diseases. I look up to Him when I am sick. I look up to Him as the one who will make me whole. I don't put my trust in drugs, therapies or any other thing; even though it is not a sin (I am not against the use of medication). So accept Christ as your healer as you accepted Him as your savior. David accepted God as His healer and said in Psalm 103:3:

> *"Who forgiveth all thine iniquities; who healeth all thy diseases;"*

We surely know that there's no healer like Christ. He is "The Healer". When He was on earth, healing constituted most part of His ministry. In Acts 10:38, Peter, in his own way of summarizing the ministry of Jesus, said:

> *"How God anointed Jesus of Nazareth with the Holy Ghost and with power: who went about doing good, and healing all that were oppressed of the devil; for God was with him."*

We see this also in Matthew 4:23:

> *"And Jesus went about all Galilee, teaching in their synagogues, and preaching the gospel of the kingdom, and healing all manner of sickness and all manner of disease among the people."*

Jesus took healing seriously when He was on earth; and even though we cannot see Him physically right now, the person of the Holy Spirit is still with us. Jesus' presence is still in our midst; because wherever the Holy Spirit is found, Jesus is found there. The Holy Spirit is the Spirit of Christ. The same Spirit that anointed Jesus, the same Spirit by whom Jesus healed people, is the same Spirit He has sent to represent Him.

So accept Christ as your healer, regardless of what the doctor says and no matter how bad the condition is. Whatever symptom you may have in your body, do not be afraid.

I don't like a pattern I see very often in the healing line - people avoid checking something out at the doctor's, due to fear of a negative or bad report. Medical science says there's no hope, and fear grips; but not when Jesus Christ is your doctor! Maybe the word *"healer"* is the problem, so accept Jesus as your doctor. There are things the doctors of this world can cure and there are other problems they cannot cure; but not Christ Jesus. Jesus can cure all diseases.

> *"And Jesus went about all the cities and villages, teaching in their synagogues, and preaching the gospel of the kingdom, and healing every sickness and every disease among the people."*
> **Matthew 9:35**

Jesus went about Galilee healing every sickness and every disease among the people. No sickness or disease is too tough for Him to handle; whether medical science can heal it or not. So the reason why we hear such news and a sense of gloom comes over us is because our trust is not in Christ. We have not accepted Him as healer, but look up to medical doctors as our healer.

The foundation to receiving healing from God is to accept Christ as your healer. Even when you still need medication or therapy, decide to look beyond it to God; but God can heal without drugs. There is nothing He cannot heal. So never let anything move you. No news or evil report should ever move you.

Last year, a woman with ovarian cancer shared this testimony in church. Having been abandoned by her husband, she couldn't tell her children about the situation. She also did not want to scare her siblings, so she decided not to tell anybody; not even her pastors. But there was a particular service we had on a Sunday evening and she just believed God for her healing. She made that service her point of contact and she received her healing by faith. She said "I left believing that I was healed." Five days later, she noticed that the symptoms had disappeared from her body and she went to the hospital to check. The doctors were mesmerized. They ran four tests on her but the cancer was nowhere to be found. She had accepted Jesus as her healer.

There is nothing God cannot do. No matter what the doctor says, don't be afraid: He is the mighty healer.

2.   Confess any known sin.

Sin breaks fellowship with God; so we should promptly reunite with God when we fall into sin.

"Neither give place to the devil".
Ephesians 4:27

This means that despite the efficiency of the blood of Jesus to cover all our sins, a sin that is un-repented of, is not yet under the blood. It is when we confess our sins that He is faithful and just to forgive us and to cleanse us from all unrighteousness (1 John 1:9). The power of the blood is only activated upon our confession of sin. It is repentance that brings the new act under the blood. So confess any known sin.

3.   Forgive any offender. (Mark 11:25; Matthew 6:12; 14-15, James 5:15-16, Job 42:10).

It is very clear from the above scriptures that offences hinder prayer and negate our faith. Whereas forgiveness of one another's offences release the healing power of God to restore us back to health.

Let go of hurts and bitterness you are holding onto and the power of God will flow unhindered to heal you.

4.   Claim your healing by faith (in prayer). (Mark 11: 24, John 14:13-14).

The concept of "asking ", as introduced by the Lord Jesus, is that of "demanding as of right". Of course in Romans 8:15-17, the reality of our sonship is clear. As sons, we have God as our "Abba" - whose modern equivalent will be the English word "Daddy". As children, we are heirs of God and joint heirs with Christ. This brings us into the sonship status of Christ with the father, conferring on us the right to make demands as of rightful heirs from the father.

Again in Matthew 15:22-28, Jesus in His conversation with

the Syrophenician woman, tells her it was improper for Him to give the children's bread to the dogs – "children" here refers to the children of the covenant Israel. As New Testament Covenant children, we are entitled to "our bread". We therefore should claim it when we need it.

5.   Confess your healing.

After asking in prayer, we are to change our confession from that of sickness to that of healing.

> *Therefore I say unto you, What things soever ye desire, when ye pray, believe that ye receive them, and ye shall have them.*
> **Mark 11:24**

We are to believe that we received when we pray. After praying, our speech should reflect that we know we have received, even in the face of contrary symptoms. Some have misunderstood that to mean a denial of their physical condition, which is only tantamount to lying. However, a continued declaration of the reality only reinforces it and weakens our faith. Statements like "I believe I am healed", "I am getting better", "I am strong" and others that are in line with our faith should follow prayer.

6.   Start praising God.

Gratitude and praise are a great part of the expression of our faith in God.

We are encouraged to end prayer with thanksgiving and praise in the "model prayer" that Jesus taught His disciples to pray.

> *...For thine is the kingdom, and the power, and the glory, for ever. Amen.*
> **Matthew 6:13**

Again, concerning our worries, we are to pray with thanksgiving (Philippians 4:6). This proper ending of our prayer should be continued till our healings manifest in our experience.

7.   Act like you're healed.

We ought to act in correspondence with our faith, because faith without works (corresponding actions) is dead. (James 2:20). It has been quite controversial discussing what constitutes corresponding action or not. But from my personal experience and what is exemplified in the earthly ministry of our Lord Jesus Christ, I believe anything we do that demonstrates an expectation of relief from the symptoms of sickness is faith. This could range from a blind man going to wash in the pool (John chapter 9), lepers going to testify (Luke 17:14) or a man with a withered hand making efforts to stretch it at the Lord's command (Matthew 12:13). What you do to demonstrate your faith should be determined by your "level of faith".

Medical treatment does not negate faith, even if it is a demonstration of a lower level of faith than going without it at all. Submitting to surgery does not negate faith; however it is a demonstration of a lower level of faith. Do what you can CONFIDENTLY do without fear and doubt. Some have acted beyond their levels of faith to conform to religious norms, impress others or simply out of fear of surgery. All of that is presumption or foolishness.

We should however continue to build our faith, so our dependence on God can be total. Reliance on medical science itself removes the touch of the supernatural from our lives and limits our access to God's abundant provision.

"Healed people ought not to be lying down on the bed", the still small voice of the Holy Spirit spoke from within me. I was on the verge of giving up one week, after holding on to the word of God alone and refusing to get medical help. In my frustration, I cried for God's mercy, but the still small voice spoke up within me saying "The just shall live by faith". My tears were an expression of a failing and weakening faith. What followed was "Healed people ought not to be lying down on the bed". I stood up and dressed for a birthday anniversary celebration. I was dancing at the celebration when I remembered, "I ought to be sick". God had honored corresponding action as the symptoms of malaria fever had left me.

While I have at times (out of impatience) taken drugs over the years, the lesson of that day was not lost on me and I have received healing many times without involving medical science at all. So act in line with God's word and continue to do so till you see manifestation.

Chapter 4
Healing is God's Will

Proof That God Wants You Well

"But he was wounded for our transgressions; he was bruised for our iniquities: the chastisement of our peace was upon him; and with his stripes we are healed."
Isaiah 53:5

"Who his own self bare our sins in his own body on the tree, that we, being dead to sins, should live unto righteousness: by whose stripes ye were healed."
1 Peter 2:24

Some have taken the position that it is God's will to afflict us with sickness and not always His will to heal us. In this chapter, I will take us through Scriptures to prove that it is God's will to heal us.

1.   God Made Adam and Eve without Sickness.
If sickness were God's will, God would have made Adam

and Eve with sickness and disease. But, we are told God saw everything he had made and "… it was good".

> *And God saw everything that he had made, and, behold, it was very good. And the evening and the morning were the sixth day.*
> **Genesis 1:31**

No mention is made of sickness and disease until after the fall of man. Sickness and disease are conditions of disrepair and malfunction in the human body. It is unthinkable that God will create something imperfect or defective.

> *And the LORD God commanded the man, saying, Of every tree of the garden thou mayest freely eat: But of the tree of the knowledge of good and evil, thou shalt not eat of it: for in the day that thou eatest thereof thou shalt surely die.*
> **Genesis 2:16-17**

> *And the LORD God said, Behold, the man is become as one of us, to know good and evil: and now, lest he put forth his hand, and take also of the tree of life, and eat, and live forever:*
> **Genesis 3:22**

That man could eat of all the tree in the garden including the "tree of life" which could have made him live forever, meant that sickness was not on God's mind for him. Sickness could take his life, but God wanted him to live forever. We find the tree of life again in revelations.

In the midst of the street of it, and on either side of the river, was there the tree of life, which bare twelve manner of fruits, and yielded her fruit every month: and the leaves of the tree were for the healing of the nations.

Revelations 22:2

Man was meant to live sickness-free and therefore healing is God's perfect will for you.

2.   God healed all Israelites at their deliverance from Egypt. In Psalm 105:37:

He brought them forth also with silver and gold: and there was not one feeble person among their tribes.

If God healed the Israelites at their deliverance from Egypt, then He will heal all of us also. It means that deliverance and healing are part of the salvation package. For just as Israel was delivered from Egypt, to go into the Promised Land, so are we delivered from the world and brought into the kingdom of God.

3.   God promised to heal all the diseases of the Jews. In Exodus 15:26:

"And said, If thou wilt diligently hearken to the voice of the LORD thy God, and wilt do that which is right in his sight,

and wilt give ear to his commandments, and keep all his statutes,
I will put none of these diseases upon thee, which I have brought
upon the Egyptians: for I am the LORD that healeth thee."

God promised them healing here and reiterated this in Exodus 23:25-26:

"And ye shall serve the LORD your God, and he shall bless
thy bread, and thy water; and I will take sickness away from
the midst of thee. There shall nothing cast their young, nor be
barren, in thy land: the number of thy days I will fulfill."

For God to fulfill our days, He must keep us from sickness. We have to live in divine healing.

4.   Jesus healed all.

This is part of the reasons why you should realize that it is God's will for you in particular to be healed. Because there was not a single person brought to Jesus that He didn't heal during His earthly ministry. When He was on earth, occasionally He would go somewhere and heal someone and then move on like we see in John 5:1-8;

After this there was a feast of the Jews; and Jesus went up to
Jerusalem. Now there is at Jerusalem by the sheep market a
pool, which is called in the Hebrew tongue Bethesda, having
five porches.In these lay a great multitude of impotent folk,
of blind, halt, withered, waiting for the moving of the water.

For an angel went down at a certain season into the pool, and troubled the water: whosoever then first after the troubling of the water stepped in was made whole of whatsoever disease he had. And a certain man was there, which had an infirmity thirty and eight years. When Jesus saw him lie, and knew that he had been now a long time in that case, he saith unto him, Wilt thou be made whole? The impotent man answered him, Sir, I have no man, when the water is troubled, to put me into the pool: but while I am coming, another steppeth down before me. Jesus saith unto him, Rise, take up thy bed, and walk.

But when people came to Him for healing, He never turned them down. And so we see in Matthew 4:23:

"And Jesus went about all Galilee, teaching in their synagogues, and preaching the gospel of the kingdom, and healing all manner of sickness and all manner of disease among the people."

Notice that He went around "all Galilee" healing "all manner of sickness and disease." So there is nothing like healing for a particular ailment is God's will and another is not. Jesus healed them all!

When gifts of the Spirit are in operation however, you find specialization with men of God. We'll touch on this later on, but you just find that some people have more results in some areas than others.

1 Corinthians 12 mentions various gifts of the Spirit, but when it gets to healing, it refers to it as "gifts of healing". It's the only one pluralized like that apart from "diverse kinds of tongues". The gifts of healing don't have just one manifestation. There are various kinds of manifestations of the gifts of healing.

So a man of God can have specialization in one area than in some other areas, but this has nothing to do with receiving healing by the word of God. This specialization does not apply to receiving healing from the word. You can apply God's word and receive any kind of healing that you want, whether the man of God is anointed in that area or not.

It is also true that the anointing on men of God do have their limitation at times, but not the anointing on Jesus; not the anointing that is on the word. For the word of God is anointed in and of itself. One time, Kenneth E. Hagin was ministering in the healing line and a particular child was brought to him who had a particular bone missing. It was a birth defect in the child. Brother Hagin, of blessed memory, had to let the parents realize that he couldn't be of help because the anointing he had was a healing anointing. The healing anointing is different from the miracle anointing.

When the gift of the working of miracles is in operation, there is creative power there. In other words, a missing part of the body can be formed. Healing is repair, restoration or a curing. It is not creative, but restorative. Healing fixes, repairs, adjusts and amends. So if there's a missing part of the body, it takes the working of a miracle for it to be replaced. So, Kenneth E. Hagin knowing that the special anointing he had was to heal, made it clear that he couldn't help. However, he let them know that if they would believe God, he could come into agreement with them, because the Bible says in Matthew 18:19 that:

> *".... if two of you shall agree on earth as touching anything that they shall ask, it shall be done for them of my Father which is in heaven."*

The parents agreed and they went into a prayer of agreement and God did it. The prayer of agreement was not based on the healing anointing that Hagin carried. It had nothing to do with the anointing of the Holy Ghost on Hagin's life, but had everything to do with acting on God's word.

When we act on God's word, we receive miracles and blessings from God. There is nothing that the gifts of the Spirit can deliver that the word will not deliver. Sometimes, this is the problem when people take sick folks to crusades for healing, and one rises from the wheel chair, but the other does not. One is healed of cancer, but another person is not healed of the same ailment. The gifts of the Spirit operate as the Spirit wills, so a person can be healed and the other not healed. It was the gift of the Spirit in operation in John chapter 5 for instance, when Jesus went to the pool of Bethesda; where there was a multitude of sick and impotent folk.

He went there, healed just one man and left. Even the man did not know Him. This was the gift of the Spirit in operation and had even nothing to do with the man's faith in this circumstance. Usually, for the gifts of the Spirit to operate, faith is needed to receive the blessing of the gift. Occasionally, as we see here, God in His mercy heals in spite of the person's lack of faith. This kind of healing is called Mercy healing.

In Lagos recently, during one of our miracle services, a man stepped out and said "I actually don't believe in miracles," yet he received healing in his body. He was converted because of the healing that took place in his own body. A lady came to Rhema Chapel, Ibadan, Nigeria on January 15, 1995 from Benin City, also in Nigeria and all she came to do was to kill her nephew (her sister's son). The mother attended church, and the sister confessed the purpose of her visit. She was a member of a marine cult, but she was healed of a waist problem she had for 6 years. Because of this she gave her life to Christ when the altar call was made. She didn't believe in Jesus before, but Jesus healed her. The gift of the Spirit was in operation there.

She didn't receive her healing through faith in God's word. She didn't know God's word; she was just a devil worshipper. Yet she received her healing. Truly, it is the goodness of God that leads us to repentance. Halleluiah! Jesus healed all.

> *"And Jesus went about all the cities and villages, teaching in their synagogues, and preaching the gospel of the kingdom, and healing every sickness and every disease among the people."*
> **Matthew 9:35**

5.   The Apostles healed all.

The Apostles also followed in the footsteps of Jesus:

> *"And believers were the more added to the Lord, multitudes both of men and women.) Insomuch that they brought forth the sick into the streets, and laid them on beds and couches, that at the least the shadow of Peter passing by might overshadow some of them. There came also a multitude out of the cities round about unto Jerusalem, bringing sick folks, and them which were vexed with unclean spirits: and they were healed everyone."*
> **Acts 5:14-16**

If Jesus alone healed all in His days, it may be easy for us to believe that it is the will of God to heal all because Jesus is the Son of God. But Jesus had gone to heaven and the New Testament church had been birthed (the same church that is still alive today, and that we are a part of).

The Bible tells us that in this New Testament church, under the ministry of the apostles, **everyone** was healed. It is certainly God's will to heal us.

We see similar results in the ministry of the apostle Paul:

"And God wrought special miracles by the hands of Paul: So that from his body were brought unto the sick handkerchiefs or aprons, and the diseases departed from them, and the evil spirits went out of them."
Acts 19:11-12

6.   There is Healing in the Atonement.

We studied this in detail in the previous chapter; that in the atoning work of Christ – when He laid down His life, and shed His blood to appease the wrath of God – there is healing.

"Surely he hath borne our griefs, and carried our sorrows: yet we did esteem him stricken, smitten of God, and afflicted. But he was wounded for our transgressions; he was bruised for our iniquities: the chastisement of our peace was upon him; and with his stripes we are healed."
Isaiah 53:4-5

"Who his own self bare our sins in his own body on the tree, that we, being dead to sins, should live unto righteousness: by whose stripes ye were healed."
1 Peter 2:24

7. Healing is God's expressed will in Scripture.

It is clearly expressed in Scripture that God is willing to heal.

> *"Beloved, I wish above all things that thou mayest prosper and be in health, even as thy soul prospereth."*
> **3 John 1:2**

Here, John was putting down the inspiration of the Holy Spirit as he wrote this letter. Also, in Matthew 8:1-3, there was a man sick of leprosy:

> *"When he was come down from the mountain, great multitudes followed him. And, behold, there came a leper and worshipped him, saying, Lord, if thou wilt, thou canst make me clean. And Jesus put forth his hand, and touched him, saying, I will; be thou clean. And immediately his leprosy was cleansed."*

This man had faith in the ability of Jesus, but what he doubted was His willingness. Jesus, however, made it clear that He was willing. He always wants to. You cannot read through the Scripture and find any place where He was asked to heal and He declined. Even gentiles asked Him to and He did: like in Matthew 15:22-28, He obliged the Canaanite woman who asked Him. Even though He told her, *"It is not proper to take the children's bread, and cast it to dogs"*, the woman said *"Yet the dogs eat of the crumbs that fall from their master's table"*. And He went ahead and healed her daughter. She was a gentile.

The centurion that came to Jesus for healing in Matthew 8 was a gentile also. He was a Roman for him to be a centurion, yet Jesus healed his servant at his request. God, all through Scriptures, clearly expresses His will to heal regardless of color or race.

8.   Jesus Christ is the same. He never changes.

When He was alive during His ministry of three and a half years, He was busy healing, conquering and delivering. Hebrew 13:8 says:

"Jesus Christ the same yesterday, and today, and forever."

If He was healing when He was alive (over 2000 years ago), He is still healing today. If God healed in the Old Testament, He is still healing today. God revealed Himself in Exodus 3:14 as **"I am that I am,"**; in Malachi 3:6, He declares, **"For I *am* the LORD, I change not;"** and Jesus also never changes. He is the same, and He is with us. He made this clear in Matthew 28:20: *"...and, lo, I am with you always, even unto the end of the world. Amen."*

9.   The Gifts of Healing.

All the gifts of the Spirit are given to meet needs.

"But the manifestation of the Spirit is given to every man to profit withal."
1 Corinthians 12:7

It is for the profit and benefit of all. So if God has given the gifts of healing for the purpose of meeting the healing needs of people, it means He wants people healed. He wants people well. It is His will that these gifts exist as proof that He wants everybody healed and well.

10.   Healing is in the World to Come.

"And God shall wipe away all tears from their eyes; and there shall be no more death, neither sorrow, nor crying, neither shall there be any more pain: for the former things are passed away."
Revelation 21:4

Like we said earlier, sickness is the inception of death but there will be no more death in the new earth, and consequently no more sickness. In chapters 21 and 22 of the book of Revelation, we're back to perfection.

In Revelation 22:2, talking about the New Jerusalem, the Bible says:

"In the midst of the street of it, and on either side of the river, was there the tree of life, which bare twelve manners of fruits, and yielded her fruit every month: and the leaves of the tree were for the healing of the nations."

There will always be healing and restoration for the nations; so you won't have to find sickness in the world that is to come. These are proofs that healing is God's will.

Chapter 5
Paul's Thorn in the Flesh

"It is not expedient for me doubtless to glory. I will come to visions and revelations of the Lord. I knew a man in Christ above fourteen years ago, (whether in the body, I cannot tell; or whether out of the body, I cannot tell: God knoweth ;) such an one caught up to the third heaven. And I knew such a man, (whether in the body, or out of the body, I cannot tell: God knoweth ;) How that he was caught up into paradise, and heard unspeakable words, which it is not lawful for a man to utter. Of such an one will I glory: yet of myself I will not glory, but in mine infirmities. For though I would desire to glory, I shall not be a fool; for I will say the truth: but now I forbear, lest any man should think of me above that which he seeth me to be, or that he heareth of me. And lest I should be exalted above measure through the abundance of the revelations, there was given to me a thorn in the flesh, the messenger of Satan to buffet me, lest I should be exalted above measure."

2 Corinthians 12:1-7

Paul borrowed an Old Testament terminology to describe the circumstance he was going through. This terminology has become a ground for many to believe that sickness can be the will of God. In this chapter, we shall examine what it meant in the Old Testament and the context of its usage in the New Testament.

Old Testament Context:

(a)   Israel was commanded to drive out all the inhabitants of Canaan.

> *"And ye shall divide the land by lot for an inheritance among your families: and to the more ye shall give the more inheritance, and to the fewer ye shall give the less inheritance: every man's inheritance shall be in the place where his lot falleth; according to the tribes of your fathers ye shall inherit. But if ye will not drive out the inhabitants of the land from before you; then it shall come to pass, that those which ye let remain of them shall be pricks in your eyes, and thorns in your sides, and shall vex you in the land wherein ye dwell."*
> ***Numbers 33:54-55***

(b)   Disobedience (of the commandments above, by Israel) will lead to those inhabitants becoming thorns in their sides. *Side* here means sides of their flesh or body; simply "thorns in their flesh". And it was a terminology that was used in reference to persistent problems. So, in the primitive world of Bible times, going into bushes for farming, war and hiding was common. Passing through them without elaborate clothing often left them with the possibility of thorns getting into their clothes or on their bodies. These thorns were quite irritating and provocative.

When I started out my life, I started out in a village. My dad worked in Ahmadu Bello University, in one of their research stations located in Mokwa, Niger State, Nigeria; but we stayed in the staff quarters located in one of its suburbs, called Ndayako. So I grew up in the rural setting, the first eight years of my life. We played around as children and went in the bush to ease ourselves. We had a little taste of primitive living. We used old car tyres as toys; and rolled them up and down the place. This took us several kilometers away from home, in nothing but our underwear. Our parents were not worried about us being kidnapped, because Nigeria was very safe and secure at that time - the rural areas being even more secure. But we interacted with the bush a lot.

Agricultural Science was a part of primary school curriculum in those days. If nothing, the Headmaster will make you work on his farm; so I was used to working on the farm as a child. Going into the bush a lot as a child, one will discover that at times thorns get underneath one's clothes or on the skin; and some of them are very tiny. They hang on your skin and are not shaken easily. You have to pick them one after the other and they can be very irritating.

So God commanded Israel as they were going into the land of Canaan, to drive out the nations already living there – to kill all of them, and wipe them out because they were ungodly nations given to idolatry and hence hated by God. This process would sanctify the land; otherwise, the ungodly nations would become pricks in their eyes. If you've ever had anything enter your eye, making you very uncomfortable, then you have an idea of what God was saying here. They represent irritating and nagging problems that persist and become difficult to solve. At times, it takes days for such dirt that enters the eye to completely clear out.

God employed the language "prick in the eye" and "thorn in the sides" to describe what the nations would become, if Israel failed to wipe them out. These nations were certainly not sicknesses and diseases. The Amorites did not represent cancer, the Perizzites did not stand for arthritis, neither were the Jebusites synonymous with rheumatism. The nations that preceded Israel in Canaan became constant problems, provoking and irritating them through idolatry, constant wars and oppression or enslavement. This was how they became pricks in their eyes and thorns in their sides.

Before they entered into the Promised Land, they had made a covenant with God. The Law of Moses was delivered to them, giving them a different lifestyle. God was the object of their worship and the tabernacle was their place of worship.

By the time they arrived in the land of Canaan, they met people whose culture and lifestyle were different. They saw people bowing down to iron, stone and other things, and it was irritating to them. When I went to Malaysia to minister a few years ago, I saw so much idolatry. I had never been so irritated by idolatry in my entire life; I never saw so many idols. There was not a single restaurant we entered without seeing the image of Buddha somewhere in the corner.

There were images of Buddha on the roofs and ceilings – they were everywhere and this was quite irritating. This must have been how irritated the Israelites felt in the face of idolatry. There was idolatry and constant war in the land of Canaan. The ungodly nations fought against the Jews over and over again, and later they began to convert the Jews to their idolatry. They oppressed them at various times and enslaved them. Israel was to drive out all these nations, to prevent them from becoming thorns in their sides but they failed to do so.

The Apostle Paul uses this language in the New Testament. The confusion most times is because he said "thorn in the flesh". When people see flesh being used in the Bible, what comes to their minds is the body. However, you will also see in the Bible a reference to the "works of the flesh." They are not necessarily the works of the body. Resentment is something you feel in your soul, so it's not necessarily the work of the body. The terminology *"flesh"* simply speaks of the sense-ruled nature; or carnal mindset. Even the word *"carnal"* used in 1 Corinthians 3 literally means *meaty or fleshy* in the Greek. Yet the things Paul described were not things that pertain to the body.

> *"For ye are yet carnal: for whereas there is among you envying, and strife, and divisions, are ye not carnal, and walk as men?"*
> **1 Corinthians 3:3**

He described envy and strife as carnal because they are works of the flesh. And the reason why the Bible uses the word "flesh" at times for such things is because the human body has five senses. And if you allow your life to be ruled by the information you get from your senses, then you're described as carnal. There is a close association between the soul and the body, that's why that language was employed. So when you see *flesh* being used in the Bible, you have to look at the context in which it is used to understand whether it's referring to the body or to the soul.

Reasons for Paul's Thorn in the Flesh
(2 Corinthians 12:1-7)

(a) **Paul had Abundance of Vision and Revelations.**
Before we even begin to suggest, reason or wonder if what we are going through is a thorn in the flesh that God permitted, the first thing is to find out why God will permit such.

Do you have abundance of visions and revelations? To qualify for this kind of thorn in the flesh, you need abundance of visions and revelations.

Paul was talking about how he had so much of these. He said he knew a man caught up into the third heavens and heard unspeakable words not lawful for a man to utter. He was referring to himself, but made a separation between Paul the spiritual man, and Paul the ordinary man when he said **"of such a one will I glory: yet of myself I will not glory …"** (verse 5). What he was saying was "In the flesh, I can't boast of anything, save to boast of what God has done in my life."

Paul's experience of paradise was so real that he couldn't tell if he went there physically or spiritually. He heard things that were beyond his time and beyond the earth. He even got revelations that he wasn't allowed to share on the earth, because in God's wisdom and sovereignty, human beings are not to have such knowledge, but Paul did. So have you experienced these? If not, you certainly don't have a thorn in the flesh.

(b)   **Paul had the tendency to become proud as a result of his supernatural experiences.**
When he came back to his humanity, he had the tendency to become proud. There are some kinds of spiritual experiences

one can have that could make a person arrogant. Because of so much knowledge and power, if care is not taken, one will no longer be dependent on God and will arrogate so much to self.

One man of God was so anointed; A. A. Allen was his name. He would get to some meetings and just say "A. A. Allen is here" and demons will just start screaming everywhere; just by announcing his presence. The Jeffery brothers were also like that; mightily used of God in the United Kingdom, many years ago – George and Stephen Jefferies. For those who haven't heard of the Kensington Temple in London, it was the largest church in Britain for many years. The Kensington Temple is one of what's called the "Elim Churches". Elim is a big denomination in many countries of the world with a lot of strength in Britain; it was founded by George Jefferies.

George Jefferies was a powerful man of God, greatly used of God in the miraculous. He had a brother, Stephen Jefferies who ministered with him at times, but he was more of an itinerant evangelist in his days. He was particularly used of God in the healing of arthritis. There were people with twisted and mangled bodies who were totally healed in Stephen Jefferies meetings.

Stephen Jefferies will arrive in a meeting and just say "Jesus is here". When he says that, miracles just break out.

Many times he didn't even need to preach before the miracles began. He would enter with tremendous anointing. While George Jefferies was more level headed, the tremendous power in which Stephen operated got him proud. He was in South Africa ministering one day when he arrogantly said "Behold today, the whole world is at my feet!" There was no nation he entered where crowds were not all trooping out to him. He ended up contacting arthritis himself. He died a cripple because he opened the door to the enemy when he allowed pride.

(c)   **God in His mercy permitted a thorn in the flesh to help keep Paul humble.**

Thank God Paul was not lifted up with pride like Stephen Jefferies, but remained humble. George Jefferies was not lifted up with pride either. The work he did is still alive today. While there were not so many Elim churches when he was alive, after him the work continued and expanded, and there are now so many of them all over the world. Shortly before he died, he had an encounter with a young man who was attending a Bible school in England.

This young man was on his way back home to Germany, when his train stopped and he had to get another train. He had a few hours, so he decided to take a walk. While walking by a particular neighborhood, he saw a house that had *George Jefferies* written on a board there.

He walked up to the house and knocked. "Is this the house of the man of God, George Jefferies?" he asked. The waiter who answered him said "Yes". "I will like to see him" he eagerly replied. When asked if he had a previous appointment, he said no but introduced himself as a Bible school student.

The waiter told him he couldn't see him because he didn't have a previous appointment. But suddenly the voice of George Jefferies came from behind the waiter, and said "Let him in". He sat down and met George Jefferies, and they discussed for about 2 hours. After about 2 hours, George Jefferies held the young man, pulled him down to his knees and laid his hands upon him.

He said it was like bolts of electricity rushed through his being. He had a powerful supernatural experience at that moment. When he stood up, he left for the train station and went back home to Germany. Shortly after that he heard that George Jefferies was dead. That young man was Reinhard Bonnke. He had an encounter with George Jefferies and there was transference of power and anointing to him. George Jefferies' ministry outlived him.

So to help Paul stay humble, God permitted a thorn in his flesh. Humility here refers to dependence upon God so that he won't be lifted up with pride. When someone becomes proud, he does not have a correct estimation of himself anymore. He thinks of himself too highly; Romans 12:3 says:

> "For I say, through the grace given unto me, to every man that is among you, not to think of himself more highly than he ought to think; but to think soberly, according as God hath dealt to every man the measure of faith."

God does not want us to think too much of ourselves. He wants us to think much of ourselves, but not too much of ourselves.

In Philippians 2:3-10, the word of God says:

> "Let nothing be done through strife or vainglory; but in lowliness of mind let each esteem other better than themselves. Look not every man on his own things, but every man also on the things of others. Let this mind be in you, which was also in Christ Jesus: Who, being in the form of God, thought it not robbery to be equal with God: But made himself of no reputation, and took upon him the form of a servant, and was made in the likeness of men: And being found in fashion as a man, he humbled himself, and became obedient unto death, even the death of the cross. Wherefore God also hath highly exalted him, and given him a name which is above every name: That at the name of Jesus every knee should bow, of things in heaven, and things in earth, and things under the earth;"

So God gave Paul this thorn in the flesh so he could remain with this sense of dependence on God. And the proof of your dependence on God is prayer. If you really rely on God, you will pray. You will go before Him in prayer and ask Him to help you. You won't do business without praying to God for direction; you will submit your business to Him. You won't do ministry without prayer either.

So your prayer life, coupled with fasting shows how dependent you are on God.

(d)   **Paul described this thorn in the flesh as a messenger from Satan.**

"*Angelos*" is the Greek word used here. It's the word used for angels. This was an angel from the devil, "sent to buffet me" he said. To buffet here means, to attack, hit or box, again and again. To understand what Paul was referring to in chapter 12, as the thorn in the flesh and the buffeting of him by this angel of Satan, we need to look at chapter 11.

Remember that the Bible was not written in chapters and verses (That's why you have to learn the law of contextual interpretation: where you find the meaning of a verse or passage in its context); it was the translators who broke it down into chapters and verses according to their own perception. Where they felt like it was a different thought being expressed, they broke it up; ended the chapter, and started another one, but imperfections have been found with this. The Bible does not tell us that the translation of the Bible was inspired by God. It was the writing of the Bible itself that was inspired by God, hence the translators' liberty to re-arrange the books. It's like 1 Corinthians 12 which teaches about the gifts of the spirit, and then it gets to the last verse and says:

"But covet earnestly the best gifts: and yet shew I unto you a more excellent way."

So it says the way to access spiritual gifts is by coveting them – meaning to desire passionately. But it says **".... shew I unto you a more excellent way"** to accessing the gifts of the spirit, and it goes on to chapter 13:1 and it starts talking about charity or love. So love is the more excellent way to the gifts of the spirit. The translators cut it off and put the love subject into another chapter, but the reality is, both subjects are in the same chapter. So we ought not to separate them in our minds when we read them. Chapter 13 was spoken in the same breath as the last verse of the preceding chapter.

We find the same thing in Hebrews 11 – what we call the hall of faith – that talks about the stories of great men and women who accomplished great things by faith. As soon as it concludes the list of these accomplishments in verse 40, in the first verse of the twelfth chapter, it says:

"Wherefore seeing we also are compassed about with so great a cloud of witnesses..."

Who are the *"cloud of witnesses"* mentioned here? All the people he had mentioned earlier in Hebrews chapter 11. So you see it's all together. We need to find out what happened to Paul in chapter 11 to have a full understanding of the reason behind his statement in chapter12.

We'll look at a few verses:

"I say again, Let no man think me a fool; if otherwise, yet as a fool receive me, that I may boast myself a little."
2 Corinthians 11:16

The same theme of *Boasting* is what continued in chapter 12 verse one when he said:

"It is not expedient for me doubtless to glory. I will come to visions and revelations of the Lord."

And also in verse five:

"Of such an one will I glory: yet of myself I will not glory, but in mine infirmities."

To *glory* means to boast. So you see he's speaking in the same breath in which he began to speak in verse 18 of chapter 11:

"Seeing that many glory after the flesh, I will glory also. For ye suffer fools gladly, seeing ye yourselves are wise. For ye suffer, if a man bring you into bondage, if a man devour you, if a man take of you, if a man exalt himself, if a man smite you on the face."
2 Corinthians 11:18-20

Here, he was talking about the way some false ministers were coming against them with the Law of Moses and were taking advantage of the Corinthians.

"I speak as concerning reproach, as though we had been weak. Howbeit whereinsoever any is bold, (I speak foolishly,) I am bold also."
2 Corinthians 11:21

"If they have any credentials I have mine," Paul implied. Notice in the beginning he had said he wanted to talk like a fool. It is foolish to start priding ourselves in the things of this life: in degrees, wealth and all of those things. It's all foolish. Even when we pride ourselves in our spiritual accomplishments, it's foolish all the same, because there is nothing you have that you were not given. You cannot pride yourself in the gifts of the spirit. Is it your family inheritance? Someone gets healed through you supernaturally; was it your property? Were you being used to heal like that before you got born again? So why act as if you didn't receive it from God? All the glory belongs to Him.

*"Are they Hebrews? So am I. Are they Israelites? so am I.
Are they the seed of Abraham? So am I. Are they ministers
of Christ? (I speak as a fool) I am more; in labors more abundant, in stripes above measure, in prisons more frequent, in
deaths oft."*
2 Corinthians 11:22-23

Here, Paul talks about all the troubles he went through,
and went into chapter 12 to explain that he has had great
supernatural experiences. He explained how much he knew
and had experienced God through the revelations and visions
he had seen; some of which were relevant to earthly ministry,
and some that were irrelevant, which he wasn't permitted to
discuss.

Because of the tendency for these things to make him proud,
God permitted a messenger of Satan to continually raise up
trouble for him everywhere he went. It was this angel of
Satan that entered into the governor who raised a whole
garrison of solders against one man. It was this same devil
that entered into people and made them beat him up many
times. In fact he was killed! In one of the accounts in Acts
of the Apostles, they stoned him to death. They ensured he
was dead before they left him. After they left, the Holy Spirit
breathed on him and he revived and entered the city again.
There were times when there was so much trouble; they had
to let him down by a basket. So this messenger of Satan was
a thorn in his flesh.

When you read Acts 16 and 17 you will understand better. This messenger of Satan was an irritating problem. Everywhere Paul went, there was trouble. It was a persistent, recurrent and irritating problem.

> *"And it came to pass, as we went to prayer, a certain damsel possessed with a spirit of divination met us, which brought her masters much gain by soothsaying: ...And this did she many days. But Paul, being grieved, turned and said to the spirit, I command thee in the name of Jesus Christ to come out of her. And he came out the same hour. And when her masters saw that the hope of their gains was gone, they caught Paul and Silas, and drew them into the marketplace unto the rulers... And when they had laid many stripes upon them, they cast them into prison, charging the jailor to keep them safely:Who, having received such a charge, thrust them into the inner prison, and made their feet fast in the stocks. And at midnight Paul and Silas prayed, and sang praises unto God: and the prisoners heard them."*

Acts 16:16,18-19,23-25

They were delivered from this situation and they moved on to Thessalonica, preaching the gospel.

> *"But the Jews which believed not, moved with envy, took unto them certain lewd fellows of the baser sort, and gathered a company, and set all the city on an uproar, and assaulted the house of Jason, and sought to bring them out to the people.*

And when they found them not, they drew Jason and certain brethren unto the rulers of the city, crying, these that have turned the world upside down are come hither also; ....And they troubled the people and the rulers of the city, when they heard these things.And when they had taken security of Jason, and of the other, they let them go.And the brethren immediately sent away Paul and Silas by night unto Berea: who coming thither went into the synagogue of the Jews."
Acts 17:5-6,8-10

But there was trouble there also.

"These were more noble than those in Thessalonica, in that they received the word with all readiness of mind, and searched the scriptures daily, whether those things were so...
But when the Jews of Thessalonica had knowledge that the word of God was preached of Paul at Berea, they came thither also, and stirred up the people."
Acts 17:11,13

This behavior was the operation of the same messenger of Satan. When you see human beings operating this way, there's a demonic force behind it. They experienced all manner of trouble everywhere they went. A child of God, however, has authority over principalities and over powers. There is no angel of darkness that should be troubling the life of a child of God or a man of God that should not obey when addressed. For once, Paul discovered trouble was being stirred up for him everywhere. He discerns it's a devil behind it and addresses the power of darkness, but his authority is defied. Who is that devil that will defy the name of Jesus?

"For this thing I besought the Lord thrice, that it might depart from me."
2 Corinthians 12:8

That's what to do when problems are naughty. You ask the Lord to intervene and take it away. But in Paul's case God said to him:

"… My grace is sufficient for thee: for my strength is made perfect in weakness. Most gladly therefore will I rather glory in my infirmities, that the power of Christ may rest upon me."
2 Corinthians 12:9

Paul was weak against this principality. Everywhere he went, he couldn't stop trouble, no matter how much he prayed. So it was not a physical weakness, neither was it sickness.

(e) **Sickness is not at all mentioned as one of the things constituting a thorn in the flesh in chapter 11.** Things like perils, judgment, death, and some other things were mentioned, but not a single mention of sickness or disease.

(f)　**Paul was weak against the *thorn* by divine permission.**

Under normal circumstances a child of God should be able to take care of any thorn he finds in his side. You should be able to arrest and stop any thorn in the flesh that rises up in your life, because you have authority as a child of the living God. You've been quickened and raised up with Christ and you're seated with Him in heavenly places (Ephesians 2:6-7). You've been given the name above every other name: the authority that no devil can defy. (Mark 16:17)

Paul must have exercised authority over angels (messengers) of Satan many times successfully, but by divine permission, he faced stubborn resistance from this one. Paul needed it so that he will continue to seek God always. When you go through situations stronger than you, you are totally dependent upon God. It was a situation that kept him humble and totally dependent on God. Stubborn circumstances keep us on our knees. This was a situation that reminded Paul of his humanity and of God's absolute power over all situations. It reminded him that he was human and not God.

(g)　**Grace was given to Paul to sustain him in that season.**

"And he said unto me, My grace is sufficient for thee: for my strength is made perfect in weakness. Most gladly therefore will

I rather glory in my infirmities, that the power of Christ may rest upon me."
2 Corinthians 12:9

God was telling Paul, "Naturally you can't handle it, but by grace you will." When He sought the Lord concerning it thrice and God spoke to him giving him the assurance of grace, Paul was assured he would survive it. So he knew even when he found himself in a shipwreck that he would survive. Even when he was adrift at sea for a day and a night, he knew he would make it; because of grace. What are you going through? Grace will put you over: there's sustaining grace to survive and to overcome. This was a season in Paul's life. When the season is over, you will find yourself victorious.

But Paul's thorn in the flesh was not a sickness or disease. Nothing in the Bible tells us so. It wasn't a sickness for the Jews when the terminology was used, neither was it a sickness for Paul. If God ever gives you a thorn in the flesh, it won't be a sickness. He does not use sickness to punish or teach His children lessons.

"Or what man is there of you, whom if his son ask bread, will he give him a stone? Or if he ask a fish, will he give him a serpent? If ye then, being evil, know how to give good gifts unto your children, how much more shall your Father which is in heaven give good things to them that ask him?"
Matthew 7:9-11

If we as humans with all our imperfections know how to give good things unto our children, will God then use a snake to whip any of His children just to make them fall in line? God disciplines, but never with sickness. Healing is God's will.

Chapter 6

How to Maintain Your Healing

It is not enough to be healed. God wants you to maintain your healing and stay strong. Below are few ways to keep yourself healthy:

1.   **Live a holy Life.**

Sickness and disease come as a result of sin. If sin brought death, then it just goes to say that if I want to live a healthy life, I should stay away from sin. If a person keeps his life holy, then he'll be fine. Remember the man in John 5? Jesus told him **"…Sin no more, lest a worse thing come upon you"** (verse 14). So to keep your healing, live a holy life. Many times, people receive their healing but do not keep it because of sin.

Neither give place to the devil.
Ephesians 4:27

Sin is a door opener to the devil that allows him to afflict us. If you keep sin out of your life, you keep the devil out.

2.   Resist the Devil.

In one of the teachings of Jesus, He said that if a demon spirit is cast out, it goes though dry places looking for rest. But if it does not find any, then it will go back to its former place. If it returns there and finds the place swept and garnished, he goes to look for seven other demons, more powerful than it is – the last state of the man is worse than the beginning (Matthew 12:43-45).

Therefore, it is very important that we realize that the devil comes back after he's driven out. So, when a particular sickness goes, it will want to come back. The symptoms will want to show up in your body again. James 4:7 says:

> *"Submit yourselves therefore to God. Resist the devil, and he will flee from you."*

So when you see the symptoms coming back, resist it. Refuse it and it will flee from you.

3.   Testify of God's goodness.

In the story of the woman with the issue of blood, in Mark chapter 5, she ended up telling Jesus exactly what happened to her. We are told in verse 32-33:

"And he looked round about to see her that had done this thing. But the woman fearing and trembling, knowing what was done in her, came and fell down before him, and told him all the truth."

She testified about what had happened. Testimonies affirm your miracle. When you say it over and over again, you affirm it. A lady in our church had a case of arthritis. I prayed with her after the service and she was healed, but few days later, the symptoms came back. When I saw her, I asked how her knees were doing without knowing that the pains had returned. She answered and said "They are fine", even though she was feeling the pains the whole time. She later told me that about 10 minutes after she said so, her knees were fine - the pains disappeared. By maintaining her testimony, she got total victory.

4.   **Live Right.**

By this I mean: eat right, exercise, and rest. We'll deal more with these later in this book. There's a lifestyle that supports divine health. Live that kind of life. When you obey God's health laws, you will stay whole and healthy. One of them is the Law of the Sabbath. It's one of the commandments you see in Exodus 20:11:

"For in six days the LORD made heaven and earth, the sea, and all that in them is, and rested the seventh day: wherefore the LORD blessed the Sabbath day, and hallowed it."

Even God Himself rested after He created everything. You are not greater than God, so you need rest.

"And on the seventh day God ended his work which he had made; and he rested on the seventh day from all his work which he had made."
Genesis 2:2

5.   **Eat Right.**

God gave food to man in Genesis 1:29:

"And God said, Behold, I have given you every herb bearing seed, which is upon the face of all the earth, and every tree, in the which is the fruit of a tree yielding seed; to you it shall be for meat."

These were the only kinds of food God first introduced/ gave to man – whole grains, fruits and vegetables. It was later that God added meat to man's diet –

"Every moving thing that liveth shall be meat for you; even as the green herb have I given you all things. But flesh with the life thereof, which is the blood thereof, shall ye not eat."
Genesis 9:3-4

Here, God gave animal protein in addition to the fruits, vegetables and whole grains He had given as food to man at first. But we should just simply follow God's priorities - Major on whole grains, fruits and vegetables and minor on proteins. That's how to eat right. We'll discuss this in detail later. Until Genesis 9, there was no animal protein in man's diet at all. God added it later and we ought to eat it in minimal measure.

6.   Fulfill Your Divine Destiny.

Follow God's plan for your life. This is a very pertinent part of maintaining your healing and having a long life. In Psalm 118:17, the psalmist said: **"I shall not die, but live, and declare the works of the LORD,"** Meaning that the purpose of living is to declare the works of the living God. If you have nothing to declare, then you have no assignment here. God is not duty-bound to protect you from sickness and disease; or to defend you against the enemy, if your life will not be useful to Him. The Bible tells us of a certain man who got a bumper harvest in a year; the harvest can be likened to a 3-year harvest collapsed into one. Rather than think of how to distribute the excess to the poor, and allow God to make him a blessing, he said:

"... This will I do: I will pull down my barns, and build greater; and there will I bestow all my fruits and my goods. And I will say to my soul, Soul, thou hast much goods laid up for many years; take thine ease, eat, drink, and be merry."
Luke 12:18-19

Our lives don't belong to us. When God blesses us with excess, it's so that we can reach out to be a blessing to others.

"But God said unto him, Thou fool, this night thy soul shall be required of thee: then whose shall those things be, which thou hast provided?"
Luke 12:20

I like the words of Paul in Philippians 1:21-25 a great deal:

"For to me to live is Christ, and to die is gain. But if I live in the flesh, this is the fruit of my labor: yet what I shall choose I wot not. For I am in a strait betwixt two, having a desire to depart, and to be with Christ; which is far better: Nevertheless to abide in the flesh is more needful for you. And having this confidence, I know that I shall abide and continue with you all for your furtherance and joy of faith;"

Paul was convinced that he would be alive because he knew his service was still needed. However, later in 2 Timothy 4: 6-7, he said:

"For I am now ready to be offered, and the time of my departure is at hand. I have fought a good fight, I have finished my course, I have kept the faith:"

His words were different. In 2 Timothy 4:6-7, he knew his

work was done and he was ready to go. So, do your work; fulfill your life's assignment, and do whatever God has called you to do. If God has called you to be an entrepreneur, get out of that banking industry and do what He requires of you, or develop a plan to do it; and when the time comes, do it. If you are called into ministry, do ministry. Whatever the call of God is on your life, do it. You don't have forever to do what you've been called to do.

> *"So teach us to number our days, that we may apply our hearts unto wisdom."*
> **Psalm 90:12**

Life is very brief. When I turned forty, my parents while conversing said: "Everything seems like yesterday". They were referring to when I was born. Forty living years to me, but it was just like yesterday to them. It's amazing how time flies.

Chapter 7
The Healing Anointing

"But so much the more went there a fame abroad of him: and great multitudes came together to hear, and to be healed by him of their infirmities. And he withdrew himself into the wilderness, and prayed.And it came to pass on a certain day, as he was teaching, that there were Pharisees and doctors of the law sitting by, which were come out of every town of Galilee, and Judaea, and Jerusalem: and the power of the Lord was present to heal them. And, behold, men brought in a bed a man which was taken with palsy: and they sought means to bring him in, and to lay him before him. And when they could not find by what way they might bring him in because of the multitude, they went upon the housetop, and let him down through the tiling with his couch into the midst before Jesus. And when he saw their faith, he said unto him, Man, thy sins are forgiven thee... But that ye may know that the Son of man hath power upon earth to forgive sins, (he said unto the sick of the palsy,) I say unto thee, Arise, and take up thy couch, and go into thine

house. And immediately he rose up before them, and took up that whereon he lay, and departed to his own house, glorifying God."

Luke 5:15–20,24–25

There is a healing anointing. Jesus was teaching, and the Bible says that **"...the power of the Lord was present to heal them"**. The *power of the Lord* referred to here is the anointing. It is the power of the Holy Ghost. But I want to draw your attention to the fact that the power of the Lord was present in this instance to heal them, and that is because there is a healing power of God.

In Acts 10:38, Peter by the Spirit of God, spoke at the house of Cornelius, *"How God anointed Jesus of Nazareth..."* Literally, the word *Anoint* means *to rub against* or *to rub on*. It means to smear something upon a surface. That's quite instructive because, if you smear paint on a wall, the wall takes on the color of the paint smeared on it. So you see the anointing of something or someone is a smearing of that thing or person. When a man is anointed with the Holy Ghost, his personality is obscured in ministry. It recedes and that which he is anointed with comes to the fore. In other words, you see humanity recede for divinity to come into manifestation. That was exactly what happened in the ministry of Jesus. Jesus was anointed with the Holy Ghost and with power; and He went about doing good and healing all that were oppressed of the devil. He went about doing good – carrying out philanthropic activities, and He was anointed to do that. But notice again the emphasis is in the verse:

"How God anointed Jesus of Nazareth, with the Holy Ghost and with power..."

The Holy Ghost executes the power of the godhead. For emphasis, *Power* was separated from *the Holy Ghost;* as if the power was truly separate from the person of the Holy Ghost. It is the same power of the Holy Ghost, but with a special emphasis. This can be seen here:

"...with the Holy Ghost and power: who went about doing good, and healing all that were oppressed of the devil; for God was with him."

With the anointing of the Holy Ghost, he did good; and then with anointing of power, He healed all that were oppressed of the devil, for God was with him. That anointing of power was for the purpose of healing, because there is a healing power of God.

"The Spirit of the Lord is upon me, because he hath anointed me to preach the gospel to the poor; he hath sent me to heal the brokenhearted..."
Luke 4:18

Notice that like there is an anointing to preach, and there is also an anointing to heal. In this particular verse, Jesus emphasizes healing the brokenhearted. That's why we have to understand that the healing anointing is the power of God that repairs broken bodies and also mends broken hearts. People's hurts and pains, anger and resentment, can also be healed by this healing anointing. It heals damaged bodies and also heals damaged souls. Many times in the ministry of Jesus, this healing power was in manifestation and people would come to him to receive healing. For instance, in Luke's gospel chapter four, this anointing was in operation:

> *"And he closed the book, and he gave it again to the minister, and sat down. And the eyes of all them that were in the synagogue were fastened on him. And he began to say unto them, this day is this scripture fulfilled in your ears."*
> **Luke 4:20-21**

In other words, Jesus was telling them that this Scripture had become reality. *"There is healing power here,"* Jesus told the people. Notice that He told the people that He was anointed. There is another account of the same story in Mark 6, where the Bible says Jesus was in His home town. But when He ministered in His home town, the people were offended.

> *"And when the Sabbath day was come, he began to teach in the synagogue: and many hearing him were astonished, saying,*

from whence hath this man these things? And what wisdom is this which is given unto him, that even such mighty works are wrought by his hands? Is not this the carpenter, the son of Mary, the brother of James, and Joses, and of Juda, and Simon? And are not his sisters here with us? And they were offended at him. But Jesus said unto them, a prophet is not without honor, but in his own country, and among his own kin, and in his own house. And he could there do no mighty work, save that he laid his hands upon a few sick folk, and healed them."
Mark 6:2-5

So the anointing of the Holy Spirit was there, but familiarity did not allow the people to receive. Because of familiarity they despised His anointing. They did not believe in the anointed of God, and for that reason, they were not able to receive, despite the fact that the power was there.

Even though both Luke and Mark did not give us the full account, when we merge the two passages together, we get a full account of all that took place when Jesus went to Nazareth. He had told them He was anointed with healing power, yet the people doubted Him. So He could do no mighty work there. He only laid His hands on a few sick people and healed them. Why? Because no matter how powerful the anointing is, one of the things you have to understand about it is that it is released and activated by faith. People have to receive it by faith and believe that it is in manifestation. Because the people did not believe, they could not receive miracles easily from Jesus.

There were times He healed people and cast out devils with just His word. He would just speak and things will begin to happen. In this case, He had to lay hands on the people; and He was only able to heal a few. In fact, the way some translations put it, it was apparent that only some minor ailments were healed. The problem was not with the power, the power could heal a whole lot. The power could perform a great deal of miracles but the people did not receive Jesus, the One anointed to heal them.

I remember years ago in January 1995, I was amazed to discover that the anointing of God upon my ministry could do more than I thought myself. I had limited myself to the kinds of testimonies I had gotten in my ministry, when I went to minister at this church in Lagos. That night, a lot of people were healed. Without any sense of exaggeration, nothing less than a hundred people came out to testify that night.

It was a church that loved to testify and the pastor said I had to take all the testimonies. There were over two thousand people in the service and we had over a hundred healed. For over an hour l was on my feet taking testimonies. Some were minor ailments while others were big troubles that people were healed of, but at the end of the line were a six year old boy and a thirteen year old girl. When I wanted to take their testimonies to wrap up the service, I discovered that they were not there to testify but they were on the line for prayer. I asked what the problem was and was told that both of them were born deaf and dumb. I was scared and said to myself, *"Look at the great service we've had here today. Satan just came to ruin the service"*. I was a little afraid, but if you are afraid, you don't show your fear to the congregation.

Pastors, even if you are afraid, don't show it to your congregation. Moses was afraid but he told the people, *"Stand still, for today you will see the salvation of the Lord"*. Then he went to meet the Lord in fear to ask for the way out of the situation. Then God told him to tell the people to go forward. When he heard from the Lord, he stood before them and told them to go forward. But he had first displayed confidence before the people. A good leader hides his issues. You don't bring your pain to the pulpit on Sunday morning. You don't go to church frowning, and taking out your trouble on other people. Be a man of God, not a *boy of God*.

Only boys take their issues to the pulpit. Men of God may have their own issues, troubles and needs, they may have challenges they are going through, but they put it at home. When they're going to church, they go in intercessory capacity, carrying the weight of the people on their shoulders and forget about themselves. What they make happen for others, God will make happen for them.

Back to the story of the six year old boy and a thirteen year old girl, I asked the people, "Do *you believe that these children can be healed*". They shouted "*Yes!*" They had more faith than I did, given the demonstration of the power of the Holy Spirit they had seen that day. And because they had faith and the power of God was there and upon me, that night I prayed for the two children. It was the girl I prayed for first. I remembered that Jesus put his finger into someone's mouth for healing, so I put my index fingers into each ear and my thumbs into the mouth and I shouted *Ephphatha*. I rebuked the deaf and dumb spirit, and the girl began to hear and speak. Don't ask me if I had faith for the second one. It became very easy.

Even I did not have as much faith as the congregation did, but because of their faith, we saw the power of God in greater manifestation. Due to lack of faith in Nazareth, the power of God that was upon Jesus to heal did not come into strong manifestation though the healing anointing was available.

"And when they had passed over, they came into the land of Gennesaret, and drew to the shore. And when they were come out of the ship, straightway they knew him, And ran through

that whole region round about, and began to carry about in beds those that were sick, where they heard he was. And whithersoever he entered, into villages, or cities, or country, they laid the sick in the streets, and besought him that they might touch if it were but the border of his garment: and as many as touched him were made whole."

Mark 6:53-56

This account in Mark 6:53-56 was in the same chapter, but it was a different experience in this place because of different attitudes. In Nazareth, only a few people were healed of minor ailments, but those who believed got the big miracles for just one reason - they believed. When the power of the Lord is present, all that is necessary is for you to believe. When you believe, you will receive and there will be a transformation.

Back to our text in Luke 5, remember that the Bible in verse 17 says: "*...and the power of the lord was present to heal them.*" Who were the people that the power of the Lord was present to heal? The power of the lord was present to heal the Pharisees and Doctors of the law.

"And it came to pass on a certain day, as he was teaching, that there were Pharisees and doctors of the law sitting by, which were come out of every town of Galilee, and Judaea, and Jerusalem: and the power of the Lord was present to heal them."

Luke 5:17

The question is: Did any of them get healed? Further down the story, we find out that none of them was. The presence of the power of God is no guarantee for healing. The Pharisees and Doctors of the law were there with wrong spirits. Some were there just to criticize and some were there with doubts in their hearts. But notice that the Bible tells us about these four men who believed. Their friend was sick of the palsy; he was paralyzed and could not get up by himself. So they picked him up.

Jesus was preaching in the house, and the house was packed. They tried to enter through the door, but there was just no way in. The man was sick, but nobody wanted to give them room to get the man in. So they sat and wondered what to do. They were desperate for a miracle. They were so sure their friend was going to be healed, if they could get him to Jesus. So they went and tore the roof. Thank God for real friends who will stand by you all the time. Thank God for those who will not leave us alone. They tore the roof and let their friend down, right before Jesus. The Bible says:

"And when he saw their faith, he said unto him, Man, thy sins are forgiven thee.
Luke 5:20

Can Jesus see your faith? James 2:20 says *"… Faith without works is dead."* Faith without corresponding action is dead.

Unless your actions correspond with what you claim to believe, it is not real faith. Real faith acts on what it believes. Real faith acts on the word of God. It demonstrates confidence in God. That was what happened here.

The same thing happened in Mark chapter 5 – the story of the woman with the issue of blood. The Bible says that the woman came in the press behind, and touched His garment. We see that story from verse 25:

> *"And a certain woman, which had an issue of blood twelve years, And had suffered many things of many physicians, and had spent all that she had, and was nothing bettered, but rather grew worse, When she had heard of Jesus, came in the press behind, and touched his garment. For she said, if I may touch but his clothes, I shall be whole."*
> **Mark 5:25-28**

Jesus was going in the multitude. Jairus had gone to Him while He was teaching a multitude, and had asked Him to come and heal his daughter who was at the point of death. He decided to follow Jairus, and the whole crowd followed Him. That's why the Bible says that she came in the press behind. It was a whole multitude. Suddenly, Jesus stopped and asked, *Who touched my clothes?*:

"And his disciples said unto him, Thou seest the multitude thronging thee, and sayest thou, who touched me?"
Mark 5:31

Jesus knew what He was talking about; despite the press of the crowd. So many touched Him, but only one touched with the touch of faith. Only one touched with the touch of expectation; and it was this woman who had an issue of blood for twelve whole years. She made up her mind that she would get her miracle from Jesus, and she came in the press behind to touch His garment. All that happened was that the woman heard that when Jesus lays hands on people, they get healed.

This leads us to the characteristics of the anointing:

1.   The Healing Anointing is Tangible.

The first thing to know about the healing anointing is that it is tangible. It is a tangible substance that can be felt, like a sweet, warm glow or heat. Sometimes it feels like bolts of electricity passing through one's body or a tingly sensation. At other times it feels like a cold chill; only that it does not hurt in any way. This power is real and tangible. It is a power that can be felt.

I started perceiving this anointing in tangible ways in June 1991. Rhema Chapel, Ibadan, Nigeria was worshipping at her first location at that time; and it would come upon me like a cold chill. In fact, my lips would be chattering as if I had cold. I would feel the heat on my skin but cold on the inside and I'll know was the healing anointing.

2.   The Healing Anointing is Transmittable.

The woman with the issue of blood heard that whenever Jesus lays hands on people, they get healed; so she used her sanctified common sense to figure out that this must mean that Jesus had healing power. The healing power flowed from Jesus to the people when He made contact with them. What's in operation here is simply the law of contact and transmission. If you bring a live wire that has electricity in it into contact with a dead one with no electricity, power flows from the live to the dead one. It is contact and transmission.

The healing power of God, like electricity, is transmittable. That's why all you need to do is to find a point of contact for the anointing. The woman figured out that if Jesus laid hands on people and they get their healing, it must be that the power of God is transmitted from Jesus into their bodies. That means the important thing is contact. It does not matter if it is Jesus laying His hands on them, or they are the ones laying their hands on Him. She figured out that the important thing was contact and transmission. It did not matter who touched who.

She then took her sanctified common sense deeper. She reasoned that it was not just a matter of touching Him.

Since whatever touches him gets the power, then the garment that is touching Him must be anointed too. That's why ministers of the gospel sometimes minister with their jackets.

The same thing happened in 2 Kings Chapter 2. Elisha wanted a double portion of Elijah's anointing, and Elijah dropped his mantle when he was being caught up into heaven. That was all Elisha saw; so he took that garment. He knew it was symbolic. The garment was saying that the spirit of Elijah was upon him, but that anointing was present in the garment.

So he went to the waters of the Jordan. Elisha could never part the waters of the Jordan into two before then. Elijah had parted the waters for both of them when they were going over, but the water had closed up again. So Elisha took the garment and smote the waters of the Jordan, and said "*Where is the lord God of Elijah?*" and the waters parted into two. That anointing was on the mantle.

The woman with the issue of blood figured must have said to herself, "*Since the power would be on whatever is touching Him then I don't need to touch him. All I need is to touch something that is touching him (his clothes); and it's the same thing as he laying his hands on me.* So she came in the press and touched His clothes. Once she made contact with His garment; that was it.

The power flowed into her body because she believed it and she was healed. With the healing anointing all you need to do is to make contact.

There was a teaching – a book by Paul Tan - that I came across in 1994. I came across this book in Nairobi, Kenya and I've not seen it since then. It's titled *The Anointing of the Holy Ghost*. I saw it in someone's house, read it and the author brought something out about electricity that is so true. When voltage is very high, current leaps through the air. If you've ever found yourself under a high tension mast of cables before, you'll notice a tingly sensation in your body, when passing under it. It gives a kind of sound because electric current is passing through you, even though you're not making direct contact with the wire. Of course, at the point of direct contact, it can kill right away. But when you come within a certain distance of that electric high tension cable, you can feel the current because the current is leaping through the air. That is why a man of God can be ministering at the front of an auditorium and someone is falling under the anointing at the back.

Look at when voltage was very high in Acts 5:14-16:

"And believers were the more added to the Lord, multitudes both of men and women. Insomuch that they brought forth the sick into the streets, and laid them on beds and couches, that at

the least the shadow of Peter passing by might overshadow some of them. There came also a multitude out of the cities round about unto Jerusalem, bringing sick folks, and them which were vexed with unclean spirits: and they were healed everyone."

Notice verse 15: *"...that at the least the shadow of Peter passing by..."* In the story we read about the ministry of Jesus in Mark 6, they laid on the streets to touch the hem of his garment. In the story of Peter, it had moved higher. It was not a matter of touching Peter's clothes; it was a matter of getting within certain proximity of Peter.

Kenneth E. Hagin said Jesus told him, *"When the anointing is in full manifestation in your ministry, people within three feet of you will fall, laugh or dance in the Holy Ghost".* And I've noticed that when the anointing is in full manifestation it often happens like that. Thank God for Kenneth Hagin. He helped us understand the anointing a great deal. So the anointing intensifies the closer you get to the man.

I was in Arrowhead Pond, a suburb of Los Angeles to attend a Benny Hinn Crusade a few years ago. I will never forget the experience. I knew he usually prayed for ministers in those days, on the second day of his two-day crusade meetings. When I got there the first night, I wanted to sit where ministers were seated, but I was not allowed because I did not have a prior booking. I told them that I came all the way from Africa to attend the crusade meetings, but they couldn't help me. I sat up at the balcony that first night and it was very good for me, because I was seated just over and above the wheel chair section. So I was able to observe how the *healing technicians* prayed for people and helped them put action to their faith. Right before my eyes I saw people get healed and get out of their wheel chairs.

The second morning, I knew he would lay hands on ministers, so I went to meet the ushers to please get me a seat at the minister's section. *"Oh sorry"* they said. *"All the seats have been taken"*. I said to them, *"You must find me a seat. God bless you."* So they went and talked to the head of the unit and he found a seat for me just next to the section where the ministers were seated. I don't even remember what Benny Hinn preached about that morning, but when he said, *"Ministers get down here,"* I did not just get down, I flew down.

I was already by the platform when he asked the ministers to be brought up. I was one of the first ten to get on the stairs. I made my way through the press like the woman with the issue of blood, because I knew at the end of the day, he won't be able to lay hands on everybody. When I got there, he laid hands on me, and I landed on the floor. He said *"Pick him up"*, and laid hands on me five good times. My knees were wobbling as I staggered from the platform that day, but I was rejoicing because I got what I went there for.

I saw blind eyes and deaf ears open. There was tremendous power in the house that day.

I left the arena that day and went to the house of a man of God named Bishop Anthony Willis. I went to his church to preach the day after the crusade, and we saw broken bones healed that morning. I saw a man born without an upper palate healed by the power of God. He had gone through multiple surgeries before he began to hear even faintly, but he was totally healed. I saw multiple sclerosis and rheumatoid arthritis healed that particular day. I got an impartation, but it was by faith.

I must tell you that even before Benny Hinn laid his hands on me, when I got on the platform, it was electrifying. The anointing was all over the atmosphere. It was leaping through the air all over the big stadium that could sit 19,000 people. But the air around that platform was completely electric around Benny Hinn.

3.　The same anointing that heals sicknesses drives out evil spirits.

> *"And God wrought special miracles by the hands of Paul: So that from his body were brought unto the sick handkerchiefs or aprons, and the diseases departed from them, and the evil spirits went out of them."*
> ***Acts 19:11-12***

"And ran through that whole region round about, and began to carry about in beds those that were sick, where they heard he was. And whithersoever he entered, into villages, or cities, or country, they laid the sick in the streets, and besought him that they might touch if it were but the border of his garment: and as many as touched him were made whole."
Mark 6:55-56

"And he called unto him the twelve, and began to send them forth by two and two; and gave them power over unclean spirits;"
Mark 6:7

The same power that heals the sick, has control over unclean spirits.

"And the people with one accord gave heed unto those things which Philip spake, hearing and seeing the miracles which he did. For unclean spirits, crying with loud voice, came out of many that were possessed with them: and many taken with palsies, and that were lame, were healed. And there was great joy in that city."
Acts 8:6-8

In Philip's ministry also, we see healing and deliverance going together. The same anointing that cures sick bodies, and mends broken hearts, also drives out evil spirits.

We don't need too much drama to drive out evil spirits. Pastors, don't run away from the deliverance ministry; many people need help.

4. The Healing Anointing is Storable: During a series of meetings, as I was getting ready for the service, the protocol officer assigned to my hotel suite was trying to move my face towel and the power of God just knocked him down right there.

Recently in Lagos, a church member came to me. His wife could not make it to church because she was not feeling well and he brought something for me to pray on. It was tissue paper. Usually I don't pray on such because I feel the anointing should be taken more seriously. But he asked me to lay hands on it, and for some reason, I did not object. I laid hands on it, blessed it and gave it back to him. I told him that I felt the power of God go into the tissue paper, and he said he could feel it too. The next thing I saw was that he fell, and landed on the floor under the power of God.

So we had to collect it and carefully put it in his pocket as he was guided back to his seat. I however sent someone to tell him to get it out of his pocket as soon as possible so he would be able to get home. He went home and laid it on his wife and she was healed.

There is nothing that cannot be healed; from blindness, to deafness, to cancer. Even while in Rhema Chapel, Ibadan, Nigeria I got a testimony about someone who was healed of sickle cell anemia in London, because a blessed handkerchief was sent to him. He had been bedfast for nine months, but he was healed. All that it takes is faith. The power of God is storable.

As far back as 1991 in Rhema Chapel, I remember that I was led to release the anointing into handkerchiefs during one of the services. There was this young girl who came to church; her mother had a growth in her eye and was due for operation the following week. She took the handkerchief and went and laid it on her mother. This happened on a Thursday. On Tuesday morning, the mother went to the operating theatre and the surgeons were looking for the growth but could not find it anymore. She was totally healed by the power of God. Glory to God!

I was at Daystar Christian Center to minister in the year 2000. As I prepared for the service on that Saturday afternoon, the Holy Spirit gave me a serious burden for cancer as I prayed. So I interceded against the spirit of cancer, and I got into the service. At the end of the meeting, over fifty people came out to testify about various healings that God had performed in their bodies, but there was none about cancer. So I said specifically, *"This afternoon, the Lord led me to pray about cancer."*

I asked whoever had the condition to come out. Nobody came out, but then the Holy Spirit told me that they had loved ones at home who had cancer. I asked people who had loved ones at home with cancer to come out and they did. I told them to bring out their handkerchiefs, and I laid my hands on the handkerchiefs, and prayed over them.

Two days later, a member of our church who had relocated to Lagos, and was worshipping at Daystar Christian Centre called me and said, *"Pastor, it was amazing yesterday in church."* There was a testimony of a particular lady whose sister had cancer of the breast. She got home at about 10pm, and laid the handkerchief on her sister's breast. By 2 am, pus started coming out of the breast, because the cancer had broken out in a sore. So they continued to clean it until it finally stopped coming out. He said the amazing thing about the miracle was that not only was the cancer totally removed, the wound also disappeared. There was no evidence or trace on her breasts that she ever had breast cancer.

I heard that another brother came and rolled on the platform in thanks to God. He said his father had prostate cancer, and he got the handkerchief and laid it on him.
His father too was completely healed.

It's all left to what we believe. Jesus told the woman with the issue of blood, *"...Daughter, thy faith hath made thee whole...".*

If you take any handkerchief that has been anointed home, the anointing will not leave it by the next morning. It lingers and is storable. It cannot be washed away.

> *"And Elisha died, and they buried him. And the bands of the Moabites invaded the land at the coming in of the year. And it came to pass, as they were burying a man, that, behold, they spied a band of men; and they cast the man into the sepulcher of Elisha: and when the man was let down, and touched the bones of Elisha, he revived, and stood up on his feet."*
> **2 Kings 13:20-21**

The people of God were being oppressed again by the Moabites, because the prophet Elisha was gone. These men who went to bury another man could not wait to bury him out of fear when they saw a band of Moabites approaching them, so they threw the corpse into Elisha's tomb. But the dead man came back to life when he came into contact with the remains of Elisha. The anointing had not yet left his body. The anointing lingers.

It is the anointing that heals and breaks the yoke of demons. When this kind of anointing is in manifestation, only one thing can stop demons from leaving - if the possessed person is not willing to let go:

- Because they have had encounters with the demon and don't want them to go, or

- Because they don't want whatever the demon is causing in their lives to stop. If it's causing immorality and you don't want to let go, or it's causing lying and you don't want to release it. But if your heart detests the demon, or the actions that come from the demon spirit, then with your cooperation with the power of the Holy Ghost and by believing and appropriating the power of God by faith, that demon will leave.

Just like healing, if you don't see any instant manifestation of deliverance, keep believing and confessing that you are delivered according to the word of God, and it will become a reality in your life.

Chapter 8

Divine Healing and Other Methods

We established earlier that it was never God's intention for man to be sick at all (Genesis 1: 27). Man was created in God's image and likeness; and was therefore made perfect (Genesis 1:31). There was no sickness or disease in God's plan for man. Sickness was introduced after man disobeyed God by eating of the tree of the knowledge of good and evil. There was relatively no sickness immediately after the fall, because the effect of the divine life – the presence and glory of God that man enjoyed in the Garden of Eden. This was why men lived long years of 700 and above.Reduction in life expectancy took place gradually.

Later God legislated 120 years, as the age limit for man. God never legislated anything less in Scripture.

Even though David alluded to 70 or 80 years in Psalm 90:10, this however wasn't a decree from God. It was only an observation of life expectancy during David's time.

With the shortening of man's life span and the introduction of sickness, man had to discover God's provisions for his healing. God in His mercy had made provision to alleviate the sufferings of fallen humanity.

However, of all the methods of healing that exists, divine healing is the first to be mentioned in the Bible (Genesis 20: 1-3, 10-13, 17-18).

1.   Divine Healing

Abraham was afraid that the men of Gerar might kill him, on account of his wife's beauty; so he lied that she was his sister. What he didn't realize was the trouble that would begin after the King of Gerar took Sarah, and God shut up the wombs of his entire household; and prevented them from bearing children. It took Abraham's intercession for them to be healed.

God is the source of all good things. James 1:17 says:

> *"Every good gift and every perfect gift is from above, and cometh down from the Father of lights, with whom is no variableness, neither shadow of turning."*

If there are other methods of healing, devoid of demonic interferences, they are ultimately from God; and are therefore not unbiblical in any way. God has absolutely nothing against such. However, God wants your absolute dependence to be on Him, and not on any physician or method of healing.

2 Chronicles 16 shows us how God was angry with King Asa because he sought help from physicians alone, without seeking God's help:

> *"And Asa in the thirty and ninth year of his reign was diseased in his feet, until his disease was exceeding great: yet in his disease he sought not to the LORD, but to the physicians. And Asa slept with his fathers, and died in the one and fortieth year of his reign."*
> **2 Chronicles 16:12-13**

It is wrong for a Christian to put his trust in other methods of healing, and not put his trust in God. Asa died because he didn't seek God in his sickness and disease.

The reality is that no matter what method of healing is available, they all have their limitations. Years ago while at the first church I pastored, I lost my victory over sickness and became very sickly; particularly with malaria fever. I had enjoyed divine healing for several years before then, and had never bothered with drugs.

But then I found myself as a pastor falling sick; and it happened over and over again.

I became a regular at a hospital in my vicinity, because a member of my congregation was the medical director there. I would visit his office regularly and went through series of treatments. One day I became very sick; my Senior Pastor was around on a visit, but I could hardly stay till the end of the service. I was shaking uncontrollably under the sheets on my bed.

My wife became angry at the situation. She told my pastor that she was tired of having members visit a sick pastor all the time. When my doctor was asked why it was so with me, he didn't have any answer. I took a comprehensive test and treatment at a particular time, only to fall sick again. After a while, I realized that my doctor couldn't guarantee that I would not continue to fall sick after going through series of treatments. Then I knew that medicine had its limitations, and I had to go back to God. I went back to seek God's face, and it was then that I found the answers I had been looking for. After enjoying the answers for one year without sickness or disease, I went and taught divine health in church. Praise God! I went one year without drugs or treatment.

So Asa died because he only trusted the physicians. While it is not wrong to use drugs or to seek other methods of healing, you must be careful not to put your trust in them; but to put your trust in the living God.

2.   The Use of Herbs

Someone asked a question after making an observation from Revelations 22:2 "*If leaves could bring healing, does it mean God has nothing against the use of herbs?*" The reality is that there are cures in herbs. There are healing properties in plants and herbs. When the Bible talked about physicians in the days of King Asa that we read about earlier, they could not have been but herbal physicians. In those days there was no modern medicine. The drugs of today are products of research.

The truth is, God created herbs and if there are medicinal properties in them, God put them there. There can't be anything wrong with using them to cure sicknesses and diseases. While very often we've associated these with the occult, we have to realize that the knowledge of natural herbs and teas that enhance body immunity, or contain natural antibiotics is good knowledge. God has absolutely nothing against it. I used to have problems of Irritable Bowel Syndrome and diarrhea on a regular basis without much help from drugs. However in recent times, during an extended period of fasting and prayer, I took time to do a bit of research on the web, trying to find out if there were natural remedies for it. I discovered that there were certain foods that were helpful.

God created us such that there are natural and good bacteria in our digestive tract. These good bacteria are there to prevent bad ones from multiplying and causing infections. Some of them aid in food digestion, and if you have them in limited supply, what it means is that the bad ones become larger in number. Some of these good bacteria are found in certain food substances, for instance in unpasteurized yoghurt (Pasteurization is a process of breaking yoghurt down to make it very smooth and to extend its shelf life. So most of what is available in supermarket is pasteurized yoghurt which has been rid of its good bacteria).

When I started taking unpasteurized yoghurt, I noticed that the situation reduced considerably. Another thing I found very helpful was natural honey. I also found some very good leaves like peppermint, chamomile and ginger root. The peppermint and chamomile leaves have anti-inflammatory properties; so they disallow the effects of bad bacteria on the digestive system. Proper food combination also helped a great deal.

Echinacea is very helpful for digestive troubles and also very good for sexual health; especially for women, because they are more prone to infections due to their physiology. Natural honey has antibiotic properties that fight bad bacterial in the gut. You can find *Echinacea* in some teas; at times in combination with other helpful herbs like peppermint or chamomile.

There are also leaves that have anti-malaria properties in them. While drugs have some synthetic compounds in them in addition to the useful components, most of which are poisonous, and could produce negative side effects, natural herbs are harmless. The truth is most drugs are poison. They have some properties that are not good for the body, but the good properties outweigh the bad ones. However, prolonged use of drugs - even analgesics, has harmful effects on the body. So I would rather go for divine healing or natural herbs.

3. Modern Medical Science

Advancement in science and technology has led to the development of drugs, therapies and treatments that cure or alleviate suffering from sicknesses and diseases. God has nothing against them, except when they create more harm than good. This is where you have to learn to study on your own, because there are times when some of the things you find in modern medicine are more harmful than helpful. When this is the case, you should be careful before taking the treatment.

There are several diseases that have been termed incurable, so the solutions that modern medicine proffers are rather alleviations of suffering, not a cure. In the case of HIV for instance, there is no cure for it yet. All we have are drugs that help to prevent it from blowing out quickly; and drugs that protect the infected person's immunity.

There are several other illnesses with drugs just like this, for example arthritis. These drugs however have their own side effects. So it is important to read the leaflets that come with drug packages before taking them. Read them properly. See the good things about the drug and the possible side effects.

If you don't understand your body constitution, for instance, you can get into trouble with drugs. For years I got into trouble every time I used *Fansidar* for the treatment of malaria. Blisters will just pop up all over my body, especially on my lips. It was later I discovered that it was because the drug contained sulphur. Other drugs that contain sulphur are *Metakelfine* and *Septrin*. So when you notice particular side effects or allergies when you use certain drugs, it's because something in their composition is not good for your body. Your body cannot tolerate or condone them. It will be wise to stay away from such drugs and look for alternatives. Nonetheless, I think divine healing is just the best! And the more natural you go also, the less harm you do yourself.

However, there is a bit of caution when it comes to the use of herbs. And that it's the fact that more often than not, there is no standard dosage when it comes to their use; especially the ones developed in Nigeria. There are still standards in certain countries of the world like in the U.S where they ensure that the herbs are scientifically administered. But where there is no regulation or proper dosage, we must be careful. Excessive use of even a good thing can be bad. So be a bit careful here.

In a nutshell, God has nothing against modern medicine also. It has kept a good number of people alive. One major advantage of modern medicine is that it has advanced beyond any other method of healing in the world, so it is more widely accepted. The advantage of advancement that medical science has over other types of healing is due to the well funded research that goes on in this field; plus proper education. Apart from the development of drugs for various ailments, modern medicine also affords the opportunity of testing.

Proper and regular medical check-ups and testing help you to know how your body is doing, and also helps to identify likely problem areas ahead of time. Anyone who has passed the age of 40 or from exactly 40 years of age should have check-ups from time to time. It is very important to know the condition of your body - prevention is better than cure. There are certain conditions that don't show up on time, and can only be detected through medical check-ups and tests. For example, the presence of excess fat in the blood or the liver, are very dangerous conditions that present no symptoms as a warning/sign. So anyone with a diagnosis of any of these conditions ought to be careful with overloading his/her body with too much fat and will need to cut down on a high fat diet.

Modern medicine certainly has its advantages and should be embraced where necessary. Many people have died unnecessarily. When your doctor suggests a caesarian section as opposed to the vagina delivery you believe God for, please listen. God can do what you believe Him for, but that is predicated on the level of your faith. If things don't go according to the way you would have wanted, allow the doctors to do what they need to do. After all it was God that gave them the knowledge of caesarian section in the first place. In fact, some women opt for it even when it is not medically necessary. So there is absolutely nothing wrong with this procedure.

4.   Occult Healing

For centuries, occult healing practices have existed - Voodoo healing, Buddhism healing, African native healing practices and the likes; but God disapproves of them.

> *"But the fearful, and unbelieving, and the abominable, and murderers, and whoremongers, and sorcerers, and idolaters, and all liars, shall have their part in the lake which burneth with fire and brimstone: which is the second death."*
> **Revelation 21:8**

Over and over again in the Old Testament, God warned the children of Israel not to have anything to do with witchcraft. What happens in occult healing is that demonic powers are either appeased or conjured. They are invoked. Dabbling into occult healing is entering into a covenant with satanic forces. It is idolatry. God warns in Exodus 20, *"Thou shall have no other gods before me,"* because He is a jealous God. He promises judgment on all who partake in or practice occultism.

In occultism, they have knowledge of herbs, but at the same time they also know how to conjure evil forces through incantations. Whatever thing: herb or concoction or any other thing that incantations have been rained over, don't partake of it. Don't even have anything to do with it. If you have the slightest inclination that a particular herb might have something to do with witchcraft, stay away from it. There are some of these herbal medical doctors in Nigeria that are involved with this; because when subjected to chemical analysis, their concoctions and mixtures have no footing in science. So how come they cure? They speak incantations on them, so that whenever they are used, forces of darkness can be appeased. If you beg demons for any reason, you are subject to them; in whatever way you beg them. So stay away from anything that is connected to the occult.

"Every good gift and every perfect gift is from above…" (**James 1:17**); but this excludes occult healing. The fact that people are getting well there does not automatically mean it is of God. Wherever you are asked to drink water of different colors, occult practice is involved; even if it is called a church.

If they need to burn candles around water for healing, or any of such things, know that it is occult healing. Do not go to so such places.

It is true that occult healing exists, but God disapproves of it. God however approves of herbal medicine and modern medicine; but your faith and trust should be in Him alone. Both types of healing (i.e. through herbs and modern medicine) are just ways God uses the natural to perform the supernatural. When a person is anointed with oil and he becomes well, the healing has nothing to do with the olive oil applied to the person's head. It is true that olive oil has medicinal properties, but it is not a cure for all. So if somebody gets healed after being anointed with oil, then that means it's something spiritual. It is the spiritual flowing through the natural, creating the supernatural to be a blessing. God told Naaman the Syrian, through Prophet Elisha, to go dip in the water of the Jordan seven times and then he would be healed. Couldn't God have healed him without him getting into the river? Oh sure He could have, but he chose not to. God can work through the natural to get the job done.

When I was in California sometime last year, I visited Pastor K.C Price's church with a pastor friend, and we went to check out the book store. I found a book: *"Through the Fire & Through the Water"* by Betty Price. I got my own copy and read the story again to relive its contents. She mentioned how she was led by the Lord when she had cancer, to go through chemotherapy. She prayed about it however, trusting God to perform the healing. God healed her, and the damages to her body as a result of the chemotherapy were so highly restricted, it baffled the doctors. The speed with which she recovered was also a wonder to her doctors. She had enough faith in God; so much so that when the tests were repeated a few months later, there was absolutely no trace of cancer in her body. Sometimes in the treatment of cancer, when the body is damaged, total recovery is not achieved. In her case, the cancer had reached an advanced stage; but she trusted God for a total recovery, and she recovered fully.

So always put your trust in God, so that God can work through the natural to heal you; especially when your level of faith requires that you employ the natural. But at a high level of faith, you don't need the natural at all. You can get your healing by faith all the time.

However, when the natural is necessary, don't shy away from it. Smith Wigglesworth when he was alive used to criticize some men of God who were using eye glasses, that they were not receiving their healing by faith. Eventually he needed one himself when he started aging. As great as Kenneth Hagin's faith was, he used eye glasses. These were people of faith. You really don't have to use one, but if you cannot apply your faith to get your healing, then you had better employ the natural. While eye glasses are not necessarily natural, it's another help from modern medicine. We thank God for modern medicine.

Chapter 9

Biblical Laws of Health

There are certain health laws that we can find in Scriptures. God's intent for us is to practice good nutrition. Right from the beginning, God gave man the right kinds of food to eat for the purpose of good health:

> *"And God said, Behold, I have given you every herb bearing seed, which is upon the face of all the earth, and every tree, in the which is the fruit of a tree yielding seed; to you it shall be for meat."*
> **Genesis 1:29**

Here, we see that God gave man herbs and plants for food.

He also gave him fruits and seeds. *Meat* as used here simply means food. Later in Genesis 9:2-3, God added animal protein:

"And the fear of you and the dread of you shall be upon every beast of the earth, and upon every fowl of the air, upon all that moveth upon the earth, and upon all the fishes of the sea; into your hand are they delivered. Every moving thing that liveth shall be meat for you; even as the green herb have I given you all things."

However, when we move on to the book of Leviticus, we will see that a separation was made between clean and unclean animals. While it was a law in the Old Testament, but not a binding law in the New Testament, there are however lessons to learn from them. When I say good nutrition therefore, there are a few points to note:

(a)   Major on Fruits, Vegetables, Seeds, Nuts and Whole grains. Even the animals we eat, feed from the ground. They have plants and herbs as food. There is nothing we need as far as nutrition is concerned that cannot be provided by feeding on them. Carbohydrates, proteins, fats and lipids; mineral salts and vitamins; all can be found in fruits and vegetables. So we should learn to major in them.

They are very nutritious. They are also rich in fibre. Though fibre is not absorbable by the body, it is gentle on the digestive system; and it has a cleansing effect. Most of the processed foods we eat leave debris on the gut, but fibre cleanses them out as it passes through the digestive system. Doctors usually would ask a patient to stick out his tongue, because the state of the tongue gives them an idea of the state of the patient's health. The tongue however, usually looks whitish in the morning because the body, in the process of cleansing through the night, released some toxins into the digestive tract. That is why one of the best breakfasts for you is either a whole grain cereal or just fruits. It is also usually advised that we drink water when we wake up in the morning, because it helps to cleanse the body. My wife and I at times drink green tea for its cleansing effect on the gut.

While breakfast is the most important meal of the day, you don't have to overload your system in the morning. You can take a breakfast that helps cleanse your body of the toxins released overnight and at the same time supplies the calories you need to work, without over doing it.

The foods types we've mentioned are rich in fibre, easily absorbed by the body, and are rich in natural enzymes which help in the process of food digestion and absorption. The use of probiotics for example, helped me a great deal with some of the bowel problems I used to have. Probiotics are cultured food extracts that introduce natural enzymes into the body when used. I discovered during my study, that frequent and consistent digestive tract problems may be due to wrong **food combining.**

Usually most of our African delicacies, the way we combine them consist of carbohydrates and proteins. I don't know about you, but when I eat my rice and chicken, I prefer to eat the chicken, piece by piece with the rice. It's more enjoyable that way than to eat the rice before the chicken. This also goes for any other type of food that is combined with meat, fish or any other side-plate. However, it is has been discovered that those who eat it the other way will have it digested better.

The proper way in correct food combining, is to eat the rice first, and then the meat. This is because while carbohydrates are digested by alkaline enzymes, proteins are digested by acidic ones. So when you eat a meal that is made up of either of the two, your body naturally secrets the relevant enzymes for digestion. But when you eat a combination of the two at the same time, then the two types of enzymes are secreted and they neutralize each other not making for proper digestion of food in the stomach. When this occurs, the food goes down into the large intestine undigested and it putrefies or ferments. This can lead to infections of the gut. Therefore, the rules of food combining are:

Rule #1. Eat either carbohydrates or protein with vegetables as you please, but only eat them in the same meal; one after the other. Experiments carried out with mice showed that when food was eaten from the easiest to digest (i.e. vegetables), followed by fruits, and then carbohydrates, protein and fat and lipids, in that order, after cutting them open hours later the foods were arranged in the same order in which they were eaten. So try to combine well as much as possible. Remember that vegetables, fruits, seeds and nuts were the foods God first gave us to eat, so major on these. Try to increase your intake of fruits and vegetables and decrease other processed foods.

Rule #2. Animal protein is nutritious and good for us, but don't major on them. Whole-grains, fruits and vegetables are easier to digest than protein; protein gives the body extra work to do. There is little missing in the natural, raw food that we get from plants and herbs. There are some things we get from animal protein, but most of what our bodies' need is supplied by fruits and vegetables, whole grains, seeds and nuts. When taken in excess, you need to realize that meat is very high in phosphorus, and excessive phosphorus neutralizes calcium when it binds itself to it. Hence people who eat an excessively high protein diet, are likely to have challenges with osteoporosis (a loss of bone tissue resulting in bones that are brittle and liable to fracture and infection). Again, kidney stones can form from calcium or uric acid; both of which are derived from animal protein.

While it is true that we get calcium from milk and meat, they are not the only sources. We can get calcium from vegetables; especially green-leaf vegetables. Vegetarians get the calcium their bodies' need from them. A high protein diet can cause the body to excrete calcium through the kidneys; and when calcium is in excess in the body, the kidneys try to eliminate it; but it can clump into crystals that may develop into kidney stones.

I know Nigeria is not a country where we usually have excessive protein. This is much more applicable to people of the Western world where meat is very cheap. However when we become comfortable, due to the fact that we couldn't afford it when we were poor, we tend to eat it excessively. I was at a time very guilty of this. Inability to afford more than a piece of meat per meal used to be associated with poverty, but now one piece will do just fine. In fact when I first started traveling to America, one of the things I usually looked out for was steak. But now I know better to stay away from too much of such delicacies.

In good nutrition, you major on fruits, vegetable, nuts, seeds and whole grains, and you minor on animal protein. I want to warn in particular against milk. Though it is good and has calcium, it also has a lot of cholesterol in it. Try to take skimmed milk from which the cholesterol has been extracted. I take my cereals with soy milk; which is vegetable milk and is healthier. The problem most times is that people feel these things are expensive; but not necessarily. A bottle of soy milk goes for about the same price as a bottle of Coca-Cola and it is just as expensive as full cream milk is. It is not as sweet though, but you're better off with a healthier choice.

(b)   Good nutrition majors on good fat against bad fat. Fat is needed in the body, but there is good fat and there is bad fat. The good one is known as HDL cholesterol, and the bad one is called LDL cholesterol. The cell membranes of the human body are made of lipids. Lipids are liquid fat and good lipids make for cell flexibility.

When the cell is flexible, it absorbs food nutrients well and eliminates toxins and chemicals fast. We sure take in a lot of chemicals; it is one of the bad effects of modernization. Colognes, air fresheners, some of the body creams we use; and bathing soaps, just to mention a few, all feed our systems with chemicals on a constant basis. That is why it is important to detoxify regularly because we are always exposed to chemicals in the modern world of today. The fumes of cars release carbon monoxide, which we inhale everyday as we commute from place to place. There is a lot of air pollution in our environment today; and as we inhale these things, we are taking in some bad chemicals into our system.

When the cell membranes of the body are made of good

cholesterol, they are very flexible. They are able to absorb good food nutrients excellently for your health, and then eliminate chemicals from your system. When you see mucus or pus, it is a sign that the body is eliminating toxins. All the coughing and running nostrils are actually good for the body. We most times see them as bad, but it is actually the body eliminating bad things. I'm not saying we should pray for cold or cough, but when the body is loaded with toxins, it is one of the ways the body eliminates them. Boils are also one of the ways the body eliminates poison. So for your body to get rid of wrong things properly, it's good for you to have the good kind of fat. Good fat fights infection and regulates the vital functions like heart rate, blood pressure, blood clotting; and even fertility.

One of the popularly known good cholesterol is *Omega-3*. That is why if you are not getting enough of it through diet, it is good to take it orally; especially if you are able to find it in liquid form. Vitamins and minerals are best taken in liquid form, even though getting them in this form is a bit scarce and expensive. The next form in which they are best taken is the jelly form, and finally through tablets. The process of reducing them to tablets, leads to the loss of some of their natural components, but it is still better than not having them at all. *Omega-3* is available in capsules for instance, but the best form in which you can find it is in *cod liver oil*. We give it to little babies, but we adults don't take it. Yet it is very good for us. *Omega-3* regulates sugar level in the body, thereby protecting you from diabetes. It increases body metabolism and therefore helps to eliminate excess calories: meaning that if you take the good fat, it will help you not to grow fat.

Another source of cholesterol is red meat or beef; but eat this in moderation. Take more of white meat than red meat, and even more of fish than any of the two. While some people are so disciplined that they totally eliminate both white and red meat, I would rather not totally eliminate them, so I won't feel bound. I don't like the feeling of being trapped. For instance, I have not made a law of never taking ice-cream, but I have not taken one in a long time. I know it is not good for me, because of the sugar and cholesterol from the eggs used in its preparation.

Eggs are good, but eat the yolk of eggs in moderation. For full grown adults, not more than two egg yolks in a week, because it has bad cholesterol. If you observe when you feel boiled eggs, how the yolk sticks to your hand when touched, that's the same why it sticks to your arteries. That's the character of the egg yolk, but good cholesterol breaks down bad cholesterol; so major more on good cholesterol.

Sources of good cholesterol include:
- Fish
- Olive Oil

- Sunflower Oil
- Canola Oil
- Cashew Nut
- Almonds etc.
- Safflower Oil

Sources of bad cholesterol include (take these in small measures):
- Regular Vegetable Oil
- Palm Oil
- Meat
- Dairy products
- Eggs
- Milk
- Coconut Oil

There are also other ways of handling your meat other than frying it. You can grill or roast it.

Still under fats, be careful with hydrogenated oil. The process of hydrogenation is that of forcing hydrogen into oil under high pressure, to solidify it. The margarines we have in the market were originally oil, but were turned to solids through the process of hydrogenation.

This process transmutes and changes the oil's molecular structure; and regular consumption of it can lead to obesity and weight gain. The process is carried out in order to extend the product's shelf life, but it becomes bad oil, difficult to absorb by the body. It is problematic oil that contributes to weight gain. Even those who are naturally slim need to be careful. What we eat goes into the blood stream, and when you have too much fat floating in the blood stream, then food cannot travel freely and get properly absorbed into the body. So beware of hydrogenated oil. Interestingly, natural butter in its natural state is healthy, and is available, although it is more expensive than margarine.

Another point worthy of note is to study the components of anything you want to purchase; from margarine to biscuits and drinks. Once you find hydrogenated oil there, return it back to the shelf; it is not good for you. Health conscious manufacturers are now learning how to make those that are not hydrogenated, so deliberately look out for these ones when shopping.

Let me also warn against white sugar. Sugar in its natural state is not white. When it is extracted from sugar cane the color is originally brown. For it to become white, chemicals are used to refine it. And white flour also. The wheat from which it is extracted is not white in color but brown. White flour is a product of a refining process. So if you are the kind of person who loves cakes, meat pies and other pastries, be warned. Take these things with great moderation. Their effects don't usually show when you are young.

They become obvious when you are forty but looking fifty; or fifty, looking sixty-five. You see some people still looking young and agile even in old age, and you see others going through distress and difficulty. The way the body is used and nourished in youth, is what determines what it becomes in old age; so don't take your youth for granted. Brown sugar is sold in shops and confectionaries, and is a better alternative to white sugar.

You should stay away from sweeteners also. They have some dangerous chemicals in them. Most of them contain *Aspartame;* and aspartame taken in large quantity is hazardous, especially to brain cells. Brain cells are not easily replaced; when damage is done to them, it's usually difficult for them to recover.

(c) **Drink clean water**. Be particular about the kind of water you drink. The human body is made up of 75% water. You will notice that water is so important for human life that God put a river of life in the Garden of Eden.

> *"And the LORD God planted a garden eastward in Eden; and there he put the man whom he had formed. And out of the ground made the LORD God to grow every tree that is pleasant to the sight, and good for food; the tree of life also in the midst of the garden, and the tree of knowledge of good and evil. And a river went out of Eden to water the garden;*

and from thence it was parted, and became into four heads."
Genesis 2:8-10

"And he shewed me a pure river of water of life, clear as crystal, proceeding out of the throne of God and of the Lamb. In the midst of the street of it, and on either side of the river, was there the tree of life, which bare twelve manner of fruits, and yielded her fruit every month: and the leaves of the tree were for the healing of the nations."
Revelation 22:1-2

"There is a river, the streams whereof shall make glad the city of God, the holy place of the tabernacles of the most High."
Psalm 46:4

Water is so crucial for life, so do the best you can to drink clean water. Stop drinking pipe-borne water without boiling it. I know that some of us have a solid immune system, but you are making your body fight too hard. Pipe-borne water these days is not usually properly treated. So do your best to boil your water, and filter it to eliminate the germs in it. There is so much yeast and staphylococcus in the water we drink.

A cousin of mine, while trying to introduce me to a new water purification system, performed an experiment in my house. (It is a water purification system called *Reverse Osmosis.*

Right now it is still a bit expensive but it will become cheaper in Nigeria in a few years.) The experiment that was performed made whatever impurity in the water to rise to the surface. Suddenly I saw water that was very clean and clear, coming up with two colors on the surface - brown and green. It was the borehole water of our house in Lagos. I was told that the green color stood for the microorganisms and the brown, the dissolved solids like iron, zinc, lead etc., in the water. So when we drink water sometimes, we take in a lot of metals into our bodies; and when dissolved solids are excessive in water (called hard water), it is not good for your health. I don't know if there is any simple way through which we can help that though. The *Reverse Osmosis* system however takes out the dissolved solids and the germs at the same time.

The focus really is about long term health. In fact, when some of the "good" water that we buy, both bottled and those for dispensers, were tested; the dissolved solid rating for some were as high as over 200. While that from the borehole in my house was 65, the one from the reverse osmosis system was only 15. In America, manufacturers of bottled water are required to put the level of dissolved solids in the water on the bottle. The details are put there in the UK and U.S, but for now, we have nothing like that in Nigeria.

One of the major advantages of drinking clean water is that, it helps you to think better. The brain is mainly made up of water and amino acids; so a well hydrated brain functions very well. Make sure you drink clean water and take it in a good measure every day. It's also one of the advantages you get from fruits and vegetables, which are made of mainly water. Clean water also flushes out toxins from the body. Nothing cleanses like water. That is why it is good to take good, clean water first thing in the morning.

(d) **Fast**. Learn to fast because fasting rests your body system; especially the digestive system. It takes a lot of work and calories for the digestive system to digest food every day. So when you just keep loading yourself with food, and never allow your digestive system to rest; it is not good for you, especially those who eat late at night. While you are sleeping, your digestive system remains active. That is why it is advisable to eat like 3 hours before bed time, so that the food is fully digested and your digestive system can rest at night.

Fasting does the following:
- It rests your body systems.
- It cleanses your body. The body gets into weight loss when you fast, not only because you are not feeding it with new nutrients; but the moment you cease to give your body fresh nutrients, they go into reserve. The body has reserves. Don't forget that fat doesn't only come directly from eating fatty food; they also come

from excess carbohydrates. Excess carbohydrate in the body is stored up in form of fat. So when someone goes on a long fast, the body begins to nourish itself from the reserves. It takes from between 30-80 days of not eating at all for the body to use up all its reserves. That's a lot! I can tell from experience that by the time you are abstaining totally from food, the body will be breaking down its reserve such that you'll lose an average of 1kg per day. Somewhere around the second week, it slows down to half a kilogram per day; and then you'll notice that you're losing a kilogram between 2-3days after some time. The brain just got the message to use up the reserve gradually to preserve the body. Of course you became weaker physically, but your reserve is not being depleted as fast as it was initially.

It was so exciting for me when I got on the scales each day to realize I had lost one more kilogram during a long fast. I lost a total of 20kg during my fast of 40 days, and it brought me down to my recommended BMI (Body Mass Index). The reality was that I was about 15kg above my BMI. I was pre-obese – just at the border line of getting into obesity. When you are obese, you are giving your heart too much work to do.

The heart was designed to carry a certain weight and when you gain weight unnecessarily, you overwork it.

Some people are so fat, their hearts are doing double work. Now when a thing works harder than it ought to, it usually becomes easily tired. That is the reason for fatigue. But not only that, it will pack up faster; like an abused car which won't last very long. The body that ought to last for 80 years packs up at 50, because the heart is being overworked. So it is good to fast; for your healing and for your health. When you lose the excess weight, your body is healthier.

- Fasting also leads to body repair. God designed the human body in such a way that it can repair itself when it is weary, weakened or diseased. Now a lot of what is done in medicine is to aid the body's self-repair process. Most of the repairs that the body does is done while sleeping or in a relaxed state. So fasting helps the body to repair itself. This is achieved by preserving and using the energy the body would have needed or used for food metabolism for repairs during fasting.

(e)   Adequate Rest. Like I said earlier, when you are sleeping; your body is healing and repairing itself. So get good sleep. While the body is healing itself during sleep, it is also detoxifying itself. It eliminates the bad chemicals you've taken in through creams, cologne, air fresheners and deodorants. Let me quickly mention this for the benefit of those who have issues with mouth odor. There are two reasons for mouth odor in the morning:

- Your mouth was closed overnight; so the bacteria in your mouth were multiplying faster.
- Toxins were also released into your digestive system in the process of food digestion.

That is why, if someone has constant mouth odor, usually the first way to cure it is by good oral hygiene: brushing the teeth and the tongue very well. You should brush your tongue as hard and as well as you brush your teeth every morning. Don't forget that the tongue is the part of the digestive system that sticks out, and it is a long canal that continues for a few meters. So whatever makes the tongue dirty makes the digestive tract dirty also. How dirty your digestive tract is, is part of what determines the freshness of your breath. As much as possible, you want to make sure that you cleanse and detoxify your system from time to time. In addition, good sleep also renews energy and restores the soul. Your mind is not so active when you're sleeping so it allows your brain and your mind to rest.

(f) **Detoxify Regularly.** Ideally with a good diet, you are detoxifying. However, there are additional ways of detoxifying. Other things that help to detoxify the body include:

- **Colon Cleansing.** A lot of food is absorbed into the body through the colon. So the colon at times, due to feeding on the wrong diet, no longer absorbs well because of the deposit of faeces. Overtime these deposits coagulate and harden, so the walls of the colon are laid with hardened faeces. So much so that it cannot absorb food very well anymore into the blood stream. Colon cleansing can be done in various ways. At times through enema, but I would rather natural cleansing. There are some natural herbs that help with this; basically bitters, which are probably the best. The popularly known *bitter leaf* is usually cooked as a vegetable and there are also other brands of packaged bitters. These are very helpful; even though the cleansing of the colon requires a little more than they can handle.

Enema is done in extreme cases, and doctors usually advice against doing it too frequently.

* **Green Tea.** Green tea is also very good for detoxification; especially when you take it in its original leaf form. When I travelled to Malaysia, the people condemned all our green tea bags. They claimed that the leaf is the real deal and I quite agree. Green tea cleanses the body and also has properties that numbs appetite - for those who have large appetites like I do. I noticed that about thirty minutes after I take green tea; I no longer feel hungry. Except I make myself take breakfast, I won't feel hungry until afternoon. It has properties that just numbs your appetite and helps to regulate your intake of food.

- **Fruit Juices.** Experts in cleansing and detoxification recommend a blend of certain fruit juices a few days to detoxifying the body; especially the use of lime or lemon (both in measured quantity) with water. It is very good to drink lime-water when you eat fatty food, but not the ones found in carbonated drinks. Carbonated drinks are loaded with sugar.

Do your best to detoxify your system through any of these means. Clean it out and don't overload it with the wrong things. You can have freshly squeezed orange juice or any other kind of natural fruit juice in place of carbonated drinks. Packaged fruit juices and the likes are not 100% natural. Even though the manufacturers claim that they contain no preservatives or artificial sweeteners; those drinks will not survive without any form of preservative. Orange juice cannot stand for very long without fermenting even when refrigerated.

One of the secrets to a long life is to stay as close to nature as much as possible. Our forefathers lived very long without any of the modern medical technology we have today. Reduce your intake of processed foods as much as you can. I used to be a lover of sausages, baked beans, bacon and the likes; but I have learnt to take my eyes away from them. Take your eyes away from them and don't indulge yourself; especially in processed meats which are bad for your health. Be very careful about where you source your chicken from.

Imported chicken is worse. The home-grown ones are much better. The chemicals used to preserve the imported ones and the length of time for which they are frozen, can cause the chicken to become carcinogenic at the end of the day.

So it's better to buy the home-grown ones that were not fed with artificial additives to make them grow fat quickly. They are much better because they went around picking insects and grains for food and they have lean meat. The closer you are to nature, the healthier you are.

People who live in the developed countries of the world have high life expectancy because of advancement in medicine; but they are not enjoying their lives. They experience lots of diseases and health problems because of their diet; even their young people. Most of their foods are grown with chemicals and induced with artificial hormones. There's hardly anything they eat that is not artificially induced to grow. Even their fish contain metals because of the high mercury content in their waters; and mercury is hazardous to health.

So home-bred fish is better than imported ones too, especially scaly ones like the *tilapia*. For those who love catfish, it's better to eat it without the skin. The skin of catfish is full of dirt. That's why in the Old Testament, God commanded Israel to eat only fish with scales. It is better to skin catfish if we must eat it at all; just like you should learn to skin your chicken too. While chicken does not have as much fat as beef does, it stores most of its fat in the skin.

(g)   Exercise. Walking and jogging are great ways to get your body exercised. Thirty minutes of exercise three times a week is very good for your health. Exercise has advantages that you cannot get from anywhere else; especially when it comes to the strengthening of the muscles.

Interestingly, exercise also prevents depression, because it triggers the release of endorphins into the blood stream. Endorphins create a sense of euphoria and happiness. You don't need drugs to achieve this; simply exercise. They are also natural pain and stress fighters. So exercise reduces stress.

It boosts immunity and because it allows for the shedding of excess calories from the body and strengthens the heart; it helps to prevent cardiovascular diseases, obesity and type 2 diabetes. It's been discovered from research that exercise decreases the incident of upper respiratory tract infections by 29%. These infections can be very terrible and may start just like a mild cold or catarrh; but before you know what is happening, your chest is congested, your nose is blocked and life just seems miserable.

Exercise is good for you. Walking is very good especially if you have challenges with any of your major organs - in this case try not to do heavy exercises, keep your exercises light; otherwise, exercise vigorously.

As wonderful as it is to be healed, it is far better to stay healed and healthy all the days of our lives. Occasionally, people who teach and profess divine healing are found with terminal illness and even die prematurely. Such incidences seem to cast aspersions on the integrity of the word of God whereas they are due to a neglect of some health laws in Scripture. God is never to be blamed. He has made abundant provision for our health and we should take advantage of them.

In conclusion, I would like to add that while this has not been an exhaustive teaching on the subject of divine healing, acting on God's word releases more power than amassing knowledge.

As you do something with what you have learnt, I am sure you will discover tremendous help. I do hope you will let me receive praise report from you.

About the Author

Victor A. Adeyemi is the founder and Senior Pastor of Global Harvest Church (GHC), which serves several thousands of members with church branches spread over Nigeria and the United Kingdom.

With more than 25 years in ministry, Victor Adeyemi is committed to bringing the good news of Jesus Christ and His healing power to people all over the world.

A much sought-after conference speaker, Victor Adeyemi is known for his practical approach to the Bible and has encouraged thousands to pursue a discovery and accomplishment of their God-given purpose with God.

Victor Adeyemi and his wife, Jumoke are blessed with four children and currently live in Nigeria.

About the Book

Sickness is not the will of God for mankind. God's design for us is to live healthy.

In this great book, you will discover:

- ➢ The origin of sickness

- ➢ How to receive healing

- ➢ How to maintain your healing

- ➢ How to heal the sick

- ➢ Biblical laws of health and much more.......

Get ready to live with no sickness. Rise and be healed!

The author would love to hear from you.

To contact the author, use the information below:

GLOBAL HARVEST CHURCH HEADQUARTERS
3/5 Harvester's Drive, off Liberty Road, Ibadan
G.P.O. Box 37693, Dugbe, Ibadan.
E-mail: victoradeyemi@gharvest.org
Telephone: +2347041263541
Website: www.gharvest.org

Please include your testimony of help received from this book when you write. Your prayer requests are welcome.

You can also order additional copies of this book by contacting us via the details provided here.

Other Books by the Author

- **Seeds of Destiny**
- **Quest for Freedom**
- **Taste of Freedom**
- **Turning Vision into Reality**
- **Turning Pressure into Power**

www.ingramcontent.com/pod-product-compliance
Lightning Source LLC
Chambersburg PA
CBHW020038040426
42331CB00030B/30

* 9 789784 806794 *